every **Kitchen**
tells a story

To Robyn

When I saw this I thought of
you I hope you like it.
It's your late b-day present.
Love you lots.
Nancy Lagua.

every Kitchen
tells a story

Clare de Lore and Julia Brooke-White

For my mother Moya, and the late Helen Leonard

First published 2000
HarperCollins*Publishers (New Zealand) Limited*
P.O. Box 1, Auckland

ISBN 1 86950 356 2

Designed by Jan Harris
Typeset by Pauline Whimp – PawPrints Design and Illustration
Printed by Brebner Print, Auckland

Acknowledgements

Dozens of people have contributed to this book either directly or indirectly. I wish to acknowledge and thank them. They include, of course, the women whose stories are told here. They gave freely of their time, goodwill, humour, anecdotes and, often, their food. Others, mostly friends and colleagues, helped identify subjects to interview. In particular, Karen Fisher and Rosie MacCallum provided excellent leads and contacts.

Margaret Trowbridge, Catherine de Lore, Kathryn Street and Maryanne Ahern looked after James for me, sometimes for an hour or two, sometimes for a weekend or more. I am grateful for their love and care for him.

Finally, thank you to Don for encouragement and support from inception to completion of this book. And for always doing the dishes.

Clare de Lore

Thanks to Echo and Marigold for keeping the kitchen simmering during my many absences.

Julia Brooke-White

Introduction

This book is my second baby in two years. My son James was born in February 1998 and the final manuscript for this book was delivered to the publishers exactly two years later. The two events are without doubt related. I first thought of writing about women and their domestic lives in 1996, when I left the full-time workforce. I wanted something to do, and apart from periods as a relieving producer for Kim Hill's radio programme, writing seemed the work I could most easily enjoy and manage around a lifestyle that involved frequent absences from New Zealand.

However, for various reasons the book was put on the backburner, but once James and I had spent six months getting to know each other and had settled into a routine, I thought again about the idea and decided to write about women and their kitchens. *Every Kitchen Tells A Story* is the result.

The book records the domestic lives of a diverse range of New Zealand women. To identify these subjects, I first drew up a list of well-known women who I thought would be interesting. That was relatively easy, and I was fortunate that many of them were already my friends or acquaintances, often people I had met through my background in journalism. The next and harder task was to decide who else would be interesting, and to find them. So, on a second piece of paper I wrote subject targets such as 'woman with large family', 'woman who doesn't cook at all', 'traditional farmhouse cook', etc. I spent some time in libraries looking through books and magazines trying to get leads, and sometimes this was productive. But, without doubt, word of mouth was the most successful means of identifying women to interview. Once Julia Brooke-White and I hit the road to do pre-arranged interviews, I was constantly given names to check out. Most of the women who feature in this book were quite insistent that *they* were not especially interesting, but that they had a friend who was. I still interviewed them, their self-effacing comments notwithstanding, and they were always interesting, or funny, or both. So too were their friends when Julia and I turned up on their doorsteps, often unannounced or at very short notice. It was rare to find anyone with nothing to say, and my main regret in that respect is that there just isn't room in one book for all the wit, wisdom and pathos that emerged.

Julia and I spent a lot of time on the road, usually in and around Auckland and Wellington. But I was determined that we should have a reasonable geographical representation of women, so we also visited the other main centres, as well as many provincial areas of both islands.

Our final selection of women included some who are household names, for example, Helen Clark, Cath Tizard and Kerre Woodham, but most of the people in the book are 'unknown' women. Of those who are well known, many aspects of their lives were already on public record, but very little about their views on food, family, kitchens and domestic life in general. I was curious to hear their stories, and each person revealed another side of her life.

Few of the 'unknown' women had been interviewed before or had featured in any publication. These 'unknown' women include the bubbly Pat Lee, mother of fifteen children; the delightfully eccentric Margaret Northcroft, who resigned from cooking decades ago, leaving the job to her three young sons; Gail Anset, who has turned over her kitchen, her home and opened her heart to hundreds of abandoned cats; Christine Gardiner, whose kitchen is an open steamy wonderland; and the amazingly self-sufficient mother-and-daughter hippies Wendy Medicine-Isis and Kath Wendy. There are stories, too, of how migrants to this country have successfully striven to maintain their ethnic food traditions.

Some people have asked me if I think kitchens are to women what sheds are to blokes. I can't really think of a single thing that they have in common. Sheds, it seems to me, are retreats from daily and family life, places where hobbies and dreams are indulged. They are solitary, private places and admission is by invitation only. The average kitchen is a sharp contrast. Time and again, the expression 'the heart of the home' was used by women to describe the significance of the kitchen to them and their family. Cooking is, by and large, part of their daily lives, whether they like it or not. They are seldom alone there, especially when their children are young. Often

they are juggling several activities, such as cooking, homework and feeding a baby. Some women, for example, Jane Young, even sew and work out amidst domestic chaos.

In any home, the kitchen is often the place where friends and family congregate. Sure, it's where the food and the drink are, but kitchens are seldom just refuelling stations. Conversation, gossip, humour and ideas flow freely in the relaxed atmosphere of the kitchen. Many of the women in this book commented that despite their best efforts they frequently could not persuade friends or family to move from the kitchen to the dining room in the course of an evening.

To those who might ask why this book features women only, I can assure them that I am well aware there are many men who cook well and often. But studies prove time and again that women bear most of the domestic responsibilities, including cooking, even if they are employed full time outside the home. So this book is unashamedly about women and is a salute to the incredible juggling acts that constitute their daily life. I loved meeting the women you will read about in the following pages and sharing their food and insights. Julia has expertly recorded them on film, and together the words and pictures weave wonderful stories. Bon appétit!

Clare de Lore
April 2000

Maryanne Ahern

Food should be a celebration whatever it is

Even as a toddler, Maryanne Ahern loved food and people, in almost equal measure. Her mother, Alice, says as soon as Maryanne could both walk and talk, she could be found at the front gate trying to entice neighbours or even total strangers to come in for a cup of tea. Now with a husband, two grown children and a stream of semipermanent house guests, the passion for food and people endures.

The television news producer says there is an inextricable, almost spiritual, link between food, family and friends. 'I think food should be a celebration whatever it is. It doesn't matter what the food is as long as you enjoy it — it can be bread, cheese, and tomatoes as long as you enjoy eating it together.'

Maryanne says her Lebanese heritage (she is one-quarter Lebanese) is central to her cooking.

'I just love Claudia Roden's cookbooks, both for the food and the wonderful little stories woven through the text. Through the food I cook, I want to keep our family traditions going — that's why it's important to me to make the food a celebration and to pass on this love to the children. I think we all need to know who we are and where we came from. That's why you'll find lots of things from my mother, my grandmother and her mother in my kitchen now, such as the battered old tea caddy which we still use.'

To illustrate her point, she clambers onto one of the rather rickety chairs in the room and holds aloft a beautiful serving dish, which belonged to her great-great-grandmother. 'Don't you think it's amazing that I never knew this woman, but I use the same dish she did? And her cups and saucers? It brings her alive to me and makes her a woman just like me, with all the same problems and desires. One day maybe my great-great-grandchildren will get to know me this way, too.'

Despite an admission that she hasn't consciously taught either of her two teenaged children to cook, Maryanne says she hopes they have also developed a love of food. 'I think one day I will sit back and enjoy watching them cook. But I do want them to cook, not just open cans and call that food. I can't stand all this business about pretending you've spent ages preparing a meal for friends when you've spent ten minutes and it's mostly out of cans and bottles. You shouldn't lie to friends. If you want to spend all day in the kitchen, do it, and if you want to take ten minutes, don't lie about it. I also think that cooking is quite a healing thing if you have a busy job outside the house. You can forget all that in quite a primitive way. Cooking is physical, it's hands-on.'

Maryanne's television job requires a mix of creative and technical skills and absolute punctuality. But on the home front it's a different story. She long ago gave up driving, finding it all too daunting, doesn't wear a watch and says the thing that vexes her most in her kitchen is the gas oven, which emits loud beeps and whirs when in operation. 'I don't want to sound like a complete nerd, but really, I've never discovered how the oven works. I gave up on the instruction book after five minutes, and that was fifteen years ago. I suppose I'll put up with these strange noises till the oven conks out.'

Gail Anset

It's really nice on toast, give it a try!

Feeding hundreds of hungry mouths each week may seem daunting, but Gail Anset of Pukerua Bay takes it in her stride. Gail's spacious but spartan home, currently undergoing renovations, is home to as many as one hundred stray cats — five of her own — and a couple of dogs. She runs a commercial cattery as well. Her love of cats has seen hundreds of strays and abandoned moggies sent to her, maybe more than a thousand, over the years.

She's had to abandon the idea of the kitchen being her domain — the cats dominate to the extent that she keeps the bench completely clear because the cats would spray any items to mark out territory. The floor, currently devoid of any covering, will be tiled for minimal fuss and cleaning.

Sharing her kitchen with her feline friends can get pretty frustrating, she concedes. 'Even if I go to do some baking, I can't open the fridge without all the cats coming. It's not too bad at night when I get our meal ready because I feed the cats first and they're satisfied. I find the biggest problem is the middle of the day, getting a snack — if I try to get a piece of cheese, they're full from breakfast but they all think "Oh good, something to eat!"

'It's a humungous job to feed all these cats. I've been doing this for twelve or thirteen years now and it's got to the stage where I almost hate feed times because the numbers have increased so much. People do not look after their cats, they abandon them or they don't have them neutered.

'The cats all get the same food but sometimes one of them will be on something special because of a problem or sickness. There's a pet-food place that delivers fresh food to me once a fortnight, and I use canned food. I buy for the Cats Protection League so I don't just buy a few cans, I buy a hundred cartons of cat food. I usually go to the supermarket, not a wholesaler, because their specials are cheapest.'

Gail says her cat-food shopping trips attract some funny looks. 'If I'm not in a good mood and someone comments on it I just say, "It's really nice on toast, give it a try!"'

Kylie Ayson

I love being at sea, sitting up at night, looking at the stars

Finding home ownership beyond their means proved a blessing for Kylie Ayson and her partner, Andy Billing. Kylie and Andy had been travelling the world for several years when they decided to come to Wellington to settle down. But their savings weren't enough to buy a house.

'We'd sailed home from Fiji to New Zealand on a yacht. Friends suggested we think about getting one,' says Kylie, who concedes the couple are otherwise relative novices to life on the water. A few months later they bought the 46-foot *Shadowfax*, a decision they've never regretted. 'I love being at sea, sitting up at night, looking at the stars.'

And she says the Chaffers Marina in the heart of Wellington is a great neighbourhood. 'There are about ten live-aboards and it's like a village. Everyone knows what everyone else is doing. When Andy's away people look out for me.'

With a kitchen (or, more correctly, galley) barely 2 metres square, Kylie says she's the envy of many other boaties. 'This is big, really,' she says as she surveys the interior of the fourteen-year-old yacht. 'Part of the reason for buying this boat was the spacious galley, because we both love to cook. And we have other luxuries too, such as running hot and cold water and we're on mains power when we're berthed here, but the biggest luxury is my fridge.' The stainless steel cube has pride of place in the centre of the adjoining dining area, parked under the table.

There's an electric toaster, sandwich maker, microwave oven, dehumidifier and jug. There's even a fan cannibalised from the back of a PC, to cool the galley when they make it to the tropics.

'In the year or so we've lived on board I've rarely used the oven. I would never cook a roast in there, it's too small. I don't miss it. I have two elements and usually we have something like pasta and sauce or rice and something. Two-pot meals are obviously the easiest.'

Kylie says she and Andy are planning to get in as much practical sailing experience in the next year or so in preparation for a long trip to sea. She wants to be prepared for whatever the sea can throw at her and already knows the challenges of cooking during rough weather after toughing out a storm while sailing from Fiji to New Zealand. 'You have to stand with your feet as far apart as possible to keep your balance, and just getting something out of the oven is a challenge because not only are you moving, but the oven is too. But when you are at sea for such long periods, you might as well have something with which to fill in your day.'

Sue Barrett

It's the look on the kids' faces that lets me know if I've got it right

Sue Barrett's Karori kitchen may be in need of a makeover but she couldn't care less. Sue and her husband bought the 1950s house ten years ago, believing they'd have all the time and money needed to renovate the comfortable but tired bungalow.

They'd just spent $45,000 on three unsuccessful attempts to conceive through the Australian IVF programme. 'We thought that without children we'd have the time and money to do the place up. But after all that, I actually got pregnant! We think it was the night we moved in here. So the house isn't done, but I have two lovely children,' she beams.

'I'm the chief cook. I don't mind cooking but it is harder with three meals to prepare. The kids are each allowed to choose what they'd like. It gives them a feeling of control over their lives and boosts their self-esteem. I only give them a choice of two things but if one wants one and the other wants the other, I will cook separate meals for them. And then for us.'

Sue spends more time than most mothers in the kitchen. Her initial, nervous attempt at baking and decorating son Warwick's first birthday cake was such a success, she's in demand all around her neighbourhood. 'I take about three hours and a lot of stress off a mother's preparation for a party. I'm not artistic. For the first cake I just followed the instructions in an *Australian Women's Weekly* book. Now I do an average of four cakes a week.'

Despite its old vinyl and worn wallpaper, Sue's kitchen is light and airy. She says it's a good work space for the cake decorating. 'Even though there's lots of bench space I actually tend to work on top of the stove because it's at the end of the bench. That way I get to work round two sides of the cake without moving the board. The only thing I'd change this minute would be the louvre doors on the cupboards. Have you ever tried to clean them?' she sighs.

A brand new, state of the art, drawer-style dishwasher stands out among the well-used and well-worn appliances. 'It was just one of those weekends,' she laughs. 'The waste disposal and the dishwasher both went at the same time. I was just looking out the window to tell my husband when I saw clouds of smoke and that was the lawn mower gone too. So now we have a new waste disposal too, because once you've got one, you have to replace it because of the big hole in your sink.'

As she carefully adds the finishing touches to the tenth Pokémon cake she's made in a month, she muses on the dos and don'ts, fashions and fads in children's cakes. 'I always put the candles on the board by the cake, not on it. Children don't like their pictures being interfered with. And there is no writing on the cake for the same reason.

'Trains are popular with boys, especially Thomas the Tank Engine. And I recently did Christian Cullen, the All Black, for a nine-year-old. To be honest, you and I would probably only have recognised him as an All Black, but those nine-year-olds all knew who it was. It's the look on the kids' faces that lets me know if I've got it right.'

Virginia
It's a galley kitchen and everyone loves being in it
Barton-Chapple

A gourmet breakfast is the highlight of any visitor's stay at Virginia Barton-Chapple's Oriental Bay home. Virginia, a sculptor with a penchant for vivid clothes and dangly earrings, opened her home to paying guests about two years ago.

'You would never have seen me with a cloth in my hand before I started this. It's so boring. But now everything has to be tidy and clean. It's not too difficult really.

'I got the bed and breakfast do-it-yourself book and went from there. It has the rules and regulations, and things like what sort and how many sheets you need, and what to do about money, so it was a complete package.

'Most of the time I am full. I have two nights off a week for myself, when I entertain or I just have a blobby night in front of the television. I read, or go to bed early. Most mornings I am up early, by about five-thirty. If I wasn't a morning person I wouldn't be doing this. The guest bedroom is downstairs directly underneath the kitchen. At night when the guests have gone to bed, I always set up the table and I work in bare feet so I don't make a noise on the floor to disturb them. I also have bowls

and jugs of cold water lined up because I don't want to turn the taps on in the morning in case they're in the shower.'

Virginia's not only a considerate host; she's also a very good cook and makes sure breakfast is something special. 'Usually it includes fresh farm eggs. Most people are very happy with eggs. I offer most organic fruits and I make my own muesli. I buy little frozen croissants, about a hundred and eighty-five at a time. I share them with another friend, they're great.'

While most people are easy to please, the odd one has tested Virginia's patience. 'I had a customer who was an organic vegetarian. It was very interesting,' she says, grimacing and gritting her teeth. 'It was difficult to recommend places for them to eat at night. They brought their own oats from Auckland and I provided organic fruits. They were a bit fussy, shall we say, with lots of faxes beforehand about their needs.'

Virginia describes herself as a foodie from way back. 'I used to live in England and I would have people bring things from New Zealand, like Bluff oysters. And I married a man who was a foodie. He gave me Black and Decker tools for my work, and banned me from the kitchen except to make dessert. I was allowed to make the children's tea, and then he and I would sit down to dinner at about eight-thirty. He was a writer working at home and was able to start cooking whenever he felt like it. He was a very good cook, so for many years I didn't cook.'

Apart from painting the kitchen and putting new carpet in, Virginia has done little to the kitchen. It commands wonderful harbour views and is full of works of art and paintings, including some of Virginia's own sculptures.

'It's a galley kitchen and everyone loves being in it. They always gravitate here during parties or dinners. Why? Because it's where the fridge and the wine are!' she laughs.

Janet Blair
I must be the only woman without a dishwasher

If she'd been born a decade or two later, chances are Janet Blair would have become a top restaurateur. But life has taken a different course for this thoughtful, almost reclusive, woman. For nearly 30 years Janet has nurtured a small, elegant cottage perched on McEntyre Hill near Arrowtown, coaxed the garden into an abundance of produce and raised a family of girls. She's also been cooking up a storm, in her own sublime way.

Janet speaks with tenderness about her family, food, and the cottage. 'The house was built in 1864. It has soul and I have been humbled living here. The way the women had to work just to keep the house warm — heat we take for granted. They were true pioneers. In this country there are few opportunities to live within a sense of history and I am very aware of the generations that have gone before.

'A kitchen is really a living room. You have conversation going on, children doing homework while the mother cooks. I love to cook. I had a wonderful mother who let me do anything I liked as long as I cleaned up the mess. It allowed me to develop that side of my life.

'If I had been born later, when cooking was a legitimate profession, I would have had a restaurant. But my father would have told me to get a real job.'

Daughter Janey passes through the kitchen, and can't resist plugging her mother's cooking. 'Mum's presentation is amazing. Her attention to detail for even a family meal is incredible. I often come home to an exciting meal with several different dishes.'

'One of the greatest gifts I can give to friends and family is to cook for them,' Janet continues. 'Because I have been cooking for so long, my improvisation is less hit and miss. It comes naturally to improvise. My style of cooking changes all the time. I love classic cooking, which is very time consuming. Things like slow casseroles that bring out the flavour and tenderise meat beautifully. And men love it.'

Like Janet's cooking, the Blair's timeless kitchen has evolved over the years. 'The first year we had lino put in — it's twenty-seven years old now but it has great warmth. It's the colour. I used to polish it on my hands and knees but after twenty-six years I threw the towel in and now someone comes each week to buff it professionally.'

When it comes to her surroundings, Janet says everything matters. 'I have to have things around me that give me happiness. If something offends the eye, I have to fix it; it's all about harmony and detail.'

In fact, Janet explains that despite the intimate beauty of the kitchen, full of homemade preserves, dried flowers and shiny copper pots, it's actually an exercise in compromise. 'The table needs more room. I want everything to be enlarged by two. I want couches in the kitchen. I hate the fridge. I would love a stainless steel one because I love the old with the new. Even a new one would be tucked away, though; I don't like sterile appliances impinging on me.'

A few years ago, as a 'hurry up' to architect husband John, Janet covered the current fridge in paper patterned with ancient maps. Some fragments remain. Janet has also used one side of the fridge as a place to record her favourite food-related quotes from literature.

Despite hankering for some kitchen improvements, Janet doesn't want every mod con. 'I never want a microwave oven. But I must be the only woman without a dishwasher. I want gas hobs and an electric oven. I want a pantry! It's archaic the way I live and cook. It's organised chaos.'

Kate Bristed
It was a great dishwasher except the dishes were always dirty!

When the Bristed farmhouse in Seddon burned to the ground in 1997, it was the first of a series of shocks for Kate Bristed. Kate and her daughter returned to the isolated farmhouse after a weekend away to find little other than charred ground where the house had once stood. 'It was weird. Just silence and a cool wind. It was as if someone had picked up the house and moved it.'

They lost everything, including a kitchen that was the hub of family activity. Her husband Bill and his identical twin brother Dick were born and raised in the house; Kate and Bill had raised their own three children there. All available wall space had been covered in children's riding certificates, school prizes, and family photos curling at the edges.

It was also something of a domestic appliance museum, Kate jokes. 'Bill just didn't believe in spending money on the kitchen. We had one of the original top-loading dishwashers and he'd finally gone through all the few remaining ones around

cannibalising parts for it. It was a great dishwasher except the dishes were always dirty! I'd never let myself even look at magazines like *House and Garden* because I didn't want to hanker after things I'd never have. So I found it hard coming up to speed with all the changes in kitchen appliances and having to choose from, say, sixty different models of oven. I had to think really carefully about all the decisions because I'd just never had a dream kitchen inside my head.'

When asked what she misses about the old kitchen, there's a long pause, she looks at sister-in-law Gretchen and both of them fight to suppress the laughter. 'Maybe the old lino?' Gretchen offers unconvincingly.

On a serious note Kate says she felt keenly the loss of her mother's handwritten recipe book and the children's memorabilia. But support from the community and family cushioned the loss and instead of plunging into grief, she made the best of a bad situation.

The new kitchen is laid out similarly to the old one but is lighter. Definitely more modern. The view over the paddocks and horse jumps and across to the North Island is still the same, and as cars trail up the long dusty road, she's still one step ahead with the jug already on the boil.

She laughs when she explains the bemusement of the young architect when she and Bill specified there must be a safe in the kitchen. 'He wanted to know how much money we had and how big the safe should be!'

Kate's new kitchen has renewed her interest in cooking. 'I like experimenting because of all the new stuff I have here. And all my old recipe books are gone. A friend gave me a year's subscription to *Cuisine*, which was great. After living in a cabin for a year while we rebuilt I was really keen to do some proper cooking.'

Fiona Cameron

Fiona Cameron's friends are used to singing for their supper. Dinner invitations carry a stern warning to stay away unless prepared to entertain the host and fellow guests.

Fiona entertains in somewhat eccentric style in her central Wellington cottage, which houses a superb collection of antique china. Pride of place on the kitchen sideboard goes to her grandmother's Aynsley Bluebird collection.

She says cooking and entertaining justify her china indulgence. 'If you are going to serve food, I think you should do it wonderfully or not at all, and what you serve the food in is important. I prepare lots of courses. So I get people to sing, or recite a poem or whatever from the rostrum in the sitting room. It breaks up what is normally quite a long evening!' Sometimes, a rich casserole will simmer for hours at the side of the open fire in the living room and is served up there by candlelight.

Fiona's mother is a New Zealander, her late father a Frenchman who came to New Zealand in the 1950s. 'It must've been dreadful, missing all that lovely food. He would have to go in search of the things he wanted. Mum and Dad had six of us in five years. One of the things I remember most about the family kitchen was that instead of wallpaper, my mother put up pictures of food! Whenever they got dirty or torn, she would just put new ones up.'

Once married ('I wasn't very good at it'), Fiona says there are culinary pros and cons to living alone. 'The big benefit of living alone is having a huge compost heap because I always buy too much food and most of it goes on the heap. The drawback is that you're demotivated. I love to cook, but can't be bothered doing it just for me.' She says it's a common experience for those living alone. 'A group of four of us went out for dinner recently and had a contest to see who'd made themselves the worst dinner in the previous week. I'd had toast and jam, but was disqualifed for actually cooking the toast. One of the others had eaten a tin of tuna from the can and followed it with pineapple, also from the can, but as that was two courses, he lost. The friend who'd eaten the same stir fry three days in a row thought she'd win, but none of us counted on the fourth friend, who'd demolished six red lamingtons, eaten out of the bag, while driving home from work!!

'I plan to write a recipe book quite soon. It will be called *101 Things To Do With a Piece of Toast*! But really, I can cook. The best thing I ever made was when I was living in northern France. It was a chestnut and Grand Marnier mousse. I didn't have a fridge so I just sat the dish in the snow to set. It was wonderful.'

Helen Clark

When there is time, I am quite happy pottering around cooking

For someone with little time or inclination to cook, Helen Clark looks remarkably at home in her Auckland kitchen. In fact, the Prime Minister's reputation as a non-foodie seems a little unfair. 'When there is time, I am quite happy pottering around cooking, but there isn't much chance. If I do cook, I get Peter [Davis, her husband] to buy enough ingredients for me to make two or three meals, so we have one that night, I can have some of it later that week and there's enough for some to go into the freezer. And I keep a few store-bought curries in the freezer.'

Curries are Helen's favourite food and about the only food she cooks. 'My cooking revolves around *The Complete Asian Cookbook*. I have cooked every Indian curry in it. I make them with salads that have tomatoes, onions, chilli, lemon juice and oil. From time to time I buy new cookbooks, my Italian one has been useful and I have Mediterranean and Mexican ones. But my dream meal would be a series of curry dishes, a lot of non-meat dishes, anything with chickpeas, spinach or potato; those lovely Indian breads like garlic naan.'

Helen has travelled extensively and says this has introduced her to new foods, many of which have become favourites. She's also collected some pieces of china from overseas and they're displayed in the kitchen, alongside some locally bought imported pieces. A large turkey-shaped soup tureen really took her eye and remains her favourite. 'It's florid, bold and colourful. I haven't used it that often for soup, but it is an essential part of the kitchen.'

The Clark-Davis kitchen is practical and tidy. It often doubles as an informal office, especially in the mornings when Helen's being interviewed over the phone while trying to grab a quick breakfast.

Despite her penchant for china, Helen describes herself as a minimalist. 'I don't want to have a microwave here, I don't want to learn how to cook in it. One day I will come home and I'm sure one will be here, though. Peter will just go out and buy one. And I am not sure what he thinks he would do with one if he got it!

'I am anti having things. I always ask, "What do we need this for?" I don't have a dishwasher either. Where would I put the vegetables?' she asks in all seriousness, indicating the space, happily occupied by carrots and onions, where a dishwasher would go.

'I don't believe in wastemasters, either. The waste plays havoc with sewerage and water systems. But you can't hold having a dishwasher against busy people with kids.'

If husband Peter Davis has so far lost the battle for a microwave, he's won the coffee war, and has bought himself an espresso coffee machine. Helen makes it clear the coffee machine is Peter's domain alone. 'I am terrified of it, all the steam and the hissing noises it makes. I feel the same way about pressure cookers.'

And on the topic of cooking implements, Helen laughs as she recalls the impact of a Holmes 'behind the scenes' look at the Clark-Davis kitchen, just two days after she became Prime Minister. 'Peter, by chance, got out the worst pots we have! I have had letters from people warning me about aluminium pots, I was sent a new frying pan and even my mother gave me a saucepan for Christmas. But I am feeling quite secure about my health!'

Melissa da Souza

I can cook, and when I do, I spend a lot of time on it

More than two years after completing their dream kitchen, Melissa da Souza and her partner, Burton Silver, 'still feel like kids in a toy shop'.

The two-storey wooden house overlooking the entrance to Wellington Harbour has been in Burton's family for four generations. While some changes had been made over the decades, Melissa says the kitchen was largely untouched by previous occupants. The only original thing left now is the dresser built by Burton's great-grandfather.

Melissa, a mother, publisher, writer and law student, has no regrets about the extensive remodelling. 'It was very small before. We had four kids and us and a live-in nanny, so seven people ate dinner in the tiny kitchen. It was the only room we used really. In order to get anything you wanted, you had to move people around. Our friends miss the old kitchen, which was old and junky with some modern equipment and felt like a museum. It was very cosy, but too much so for all of us every day. We both work here all day as well as living here and it became claustrophobic.'

She says she and Burton were both determined to get the makeover absolutely right, down to the very last detail. 'Before anything was built or put in we got benches and planks of wood and modelled it to make sure there was plenty of space to move around. We worked out everything with a rule. It was like theatresports.'

Melissa says they abandoned the traditional triangle planning (oven, fridge, sink) because that design rule is based on only one person working in the kitchen and that's not the case in their household.

The result of their painstaking planning is astonishingly impressive. It's a spacious, light, timber and stainless steel kitchen-cum-family room. It also exudes a charm and personality of its own, as well as reflecting the somewhat quirky, if not eccentric, humour displayed through the well-placed collections of antique implements and appliances. 'It's a bit of a lab really. We've collected things from the Hospital Board salvage stores, for example, like the morgue trolley,' she says, grinning as she pulls out a small trolley, which keeps heavier appliances like the food mixer out of the way until needed.

Other items have a more romantic, if always practical connotation. 'Every time I go into an antique shop I try to find something for Burton, especially around his birthday. The antique ham slicer was his last birthday present.'

There are lots of quirky touches. One of them is an animatronics cat, capable of being moved so it can draw on its very own blackboard. It was commissioned from Dominic Taylor, an industrial designer and inventor, and an obvious reference to Burton's runaway book success, *Why Cats Paint*.

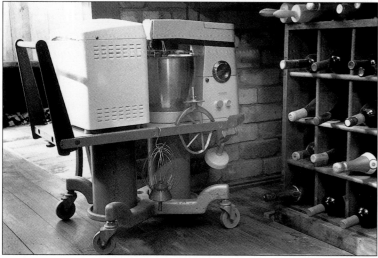

A family 'work in progress', a twisted piece of driftwood collected from the beach, is decorated with eclectic and somewhat bizarre memorabilia including a mummified rat, a monkey skull from Bali, an old eggplant, whistles, a champagne cork containing Sarah's first tooth and her umbilical peg — Sarah being Burton's daughter from a previous marriage. 'It's still being added to. We discuss the merits of what might be incorporated,' jokes Melissa.

On a more practical note, Melissa and Burton were determined to make the room family-friendly, and fun to work in. They've opted for completely open shelving above the benches. Hand-blown glass jars line the shelves. There's only one cupboard in the entire kitchen. 'We deliberately chose to have drawers for everything, so you can always find what you want, without having to reach or not being able to see what's at the back of a cupboard. All the drawers are old desk drawers with modern gliders added.'

A huge black extractor fan hangs from the ceiling. 'People keeping thinking it's an old bath and we're tempted to add an old tap to it, but it was made as an extractor.'

One of Melissa's favourite appliances is the stainless steel fridge with its own filtered-water dispenser and ice-maker. 'We can't stand the taste of ordinary water now. The only problem is that every mark shows up on the stainless steel, and you have to keep cleaning it with glass cleaner.'

The timber and stainless steel benches are probably easier to keep clean. 'The timber is just oiled, not varnished, and in fifty years these benches will have had a lot of life imprinted on them. I chop straight onto the wood at this end of the bench, I didn't want something we'd have to be precious about.'

A woodstove adds to the charm of the kitchen and also heats the house, through a series of strategically placed vents. There's a cosy seating area tucked next to the fireplace, a favourite place for adults and children alike to curl up in.

All the bricks for the fireplace came from Breaker Bay. 'Every time there was a southerly Burton would be out there gathering up bricks that washed up; we'd have piles of them around the garden. They're lovely. They have softly rounded edges. They were from the old gas works that were demolished and the bricks were just dumped in the harbour.'

A family height chart, carved into a doorframe, was preserved and moved to a new spot. It notes adult and children's heights and also records milestones such as when their daughter Francesca was potty trained.

It's a very child-friendly home and Melissa has ensured Francesca can take part in the cooking if she wants. She has a stool she can move round from bench to bench so she can reach everything she wants, especially when she and her friends make their 'witchy potions' after school.

'The kitchen works really well. Burton and I can both be in here cooking and Francesca and her friends can be pottering round in another part and there's room to do all that. The space is really important. For our Christmas party each year, we have about two hundred and fifty people, including kids, and the kitchen works a treat. There's so much room to work and to put things.'

Professional demands on both Burton and Melissa mean they don't spend as much time cooking as they might. 'I can cook, and when I do, I spend a lot of time on it. But I would spend half the day on it, so I don't during the week because I am busy and just enjoy it on weekends. Burton and I like cooking together. We are very comfortable in the kitchen together.'

Judy Darragh

I'm into nostalgia, homely kitchens, big tables

Auckland artist Judy Darragh is fantasising about her dream kitchen. 'It'll be Fifties or Sixties style, I think; more suburban comfy than anything else, with lots of plastic, lino, café curtains and formica.'

While most kitchen renovators and designers are tearing out the hallmarks of those decades, Judy is keenly collecting them. 'I even have a lino collection for my dream kitchen. There are bits of old Fifties patterns and I plan to make a mosaic of it for the floor.'

In the meantime Judy, her son Buster, and commuting partner Grant live in an old corner shop, converted to a home but looking more like Aladdin's cave. It's crammed full of Judy's treasures.

Access to the kitchen is through a 1960s clear- and blue-glass beaded curtain. The kitchen itself is barely 2 metres square, but is a riot of colour. Plastic fruit hangs

off the green walls, an old Atomic espresso-maker hogs the stove top, a collection of teapots graces the windowsills and a 1970s smiley-face light shade hangs over the black and white lino floor. 'I think this used to be the back porch originally. We never planned to be in this house for so long, but it's been seven years now.'

Judy says life on the home front was turned on its head with the arrival of Buster in 1997. 'When you are single you never cook, you're out all the time. I used to go to the supermarket about once every three months and now it's three times a week at least.'

She concedes the adjustment hasn't always been easy, but says a dishwasher saved her relationship with Grant. 'I can now understand why women get practical. I still like nostalgia and all my found bits, but there is not enough space now. We have to cook one at a time and we can't help each other in the kitchen. It was fine before Buster, but now we need space.'

Judy says despite its frustrations, her kitchen is miles superior to the one she and Grant had in their previous house, an old warehouse. 'We had a sink there, but it was not plumbed in so everything washed down into a bucket which we emptied into a toilet. We had no oven, just two rings. We've never really had a proper domestic kitchen when I think about it.'

Judy has thought a lot about women in the home and is only half joking when she says there's a male-inspired political conspiracy in the importance placed on the home and the kitchen in particular. 'Before the war women spent a lot of time at home. But post-war, after they'd worked in the factories while the men fought, they had to be enticed back with science and technology. That's why men invented things like the fridges and ovens. You spend so much money on kitchens that women are obliged to spend time in them.' But the lure of technology has yet to seduce Judy.

'I do most of the cooking. I fill my head with things to buy, I am always thinking

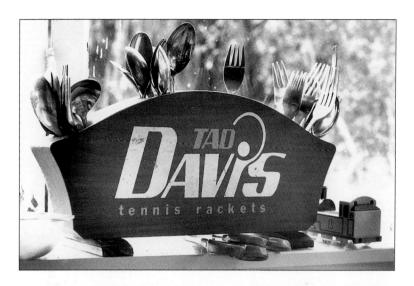

about what's for dinner from first thing in the morning. There's a feeding frenzy from five o'clock onwards. I cook Buster's meal — usually something like veges with fish fingers, or sausages, fruit — peasant food, really. Then it's the cat's turn. And I do a one-pot thing for me. You don't go to too much trouble when you are on your own. On Saturday night, when Grant is here, we go out. When I eat with friends, they tend to come over here now and bring food or takeaways with them. I like to encourage that. When Buster was four months old we had a dinner party, mostly because I wanted to prove I could. But never again. We're down to entertaining maybe twice a year. We make very good guests, not good hosts. You're either one or the other, I think. I reached my peak in Form Two when I won the Home Economics prize and then I quit.'

Judy says now, if there is any spare time, she would rather be in her studio than the kitchen. 'There's so much energy that does into food, when you think about it. Someone grows the food, then thinking what you're going to cook, going out to buy the ingredients, cooking it, serving it and then eating. Eating makes up only ten per cent of the whole exercise.'

Despite her indifference to culinary matters, Judy appreciates her small domain. 'I like the light, the sun and the views from my kitchen. And all my things I have in here make it a nice place to be. One of my favourite things is the old yellow Sunbeam mixer, which doesn't work but allows me to fantasise about making Buster cakes. And

I have cake tins with cakes on them rather than in them. The old tennis racket holder is good for utensils, and I use my colanders. I like their bright colours, rather than the plastic things you get today.

'I'm in to nostalgia, homely kitchens, big tables, lots of activity — all farmy and smelling of scones. I left home at eighteen and my first bargain was a Susie Cooper teapot for fifty cents. Being a student in Wellington, I bought mostly at the Salvation Army shop, but then found I liked old things. They're reminiscent of a happy childhood. I love my Crown Lynn dinner sets. There are two patterns — Mogambo, and for special occasions I use Napoli.'

Despite her obvious delight in her huge collection of kitsch and memorabilia, Judy isn't precious about them. 'A lot of my old china goes into the dishwasher even though it shouldn't. And I don't dust most of my things because it just comes back within a day.'

In the living area adjacent to the kitchen stands Judy's pantry, full more of things than food. China, old papers, tablecloths 'which are never used', tins that are always empty, but 'there are some basic necessities, like Weet-bix,' Judy laughs.

A 1970s mahogany cocktail fridge takes pride of place, standing on four little feet like a squared-off flying saucer. As Judy reaches inside for milk, she explains its origins. 'It was a bargain. I was going to buy a fridge for about eight hundred dollars, but it was boring and white so they said they had an old one out the back. It is one of my favourite things.'

Anne Davis
We had the garden, the orchard, and we killed our own meat

A century and a half of kitchen history can be found in one of Marlborough's most elegant homes, on the north bank of the Wairau River. Langley Dale Homestead has been in Anne Davis's family since 1851. In those days the house was part of a large cattle run, but over the last few decades the farm has been subdivided into smaller holdings. By contrast, the original cob and timber house has grown, with additions in the late nineteenth century and the early twentieth century.

Anne, who is 76, was raised at Langley Dale and, apart from boarding school days in Christchurch, it's where she's worked her whole life.

Langley Dale today is a study in decayed elegance, and the enormous kitchen hasn't escaped the ravages of time. A thick skin of aged creamy-yellow paint hangs loosely from parts of the ceiling, along with four clothes-drying hoists on pulleys that span the ceiling.

Pewter meat-covers are lined up on a wall like a hatrack, and four large water

kettles sit on one of five ovens. The original 1851 coal range is there, along with an Aga, a wood stove, an electric range and a microwave.

Despite its size, the kitchen has spread itself beyond four walls. An enormous meat safe, which Anne uses for vegetable storage, sits by the porch. There are two dairies, one the original dairy in the cob, the other in an annexe, which also houses a treasure-filled dry goods store. Old biscuit barrels are stacked alongside jars and bottles, many well over a hundred years old; its other treasures include carefully rolled up dusty remnants of all the wallpapers used in the house since it was built.

While it might be tempting to wax on about the 'good old days', Anne says life at Langley Dale was, and is, hard work. 'We are self-supporting here. We didn't run off to a supermarket to get things. We had the garden, the orchard, and we killed our own meat.

'At Christmas time, we had ginger beer and tinned fruit; we killed the chooks and it was a very special time. We'd have twenty to thirty people here when I was growing up and we've always had large numbers of people in and around the house.

'During the war, it was open house for Delta and Woodbourne. I had two brothers in the army and one was overseas. Often soldiers would arrive here, knock on the door, say they'd heard they could get a meal, and they did.'

Educated by correspondence until she was 13, Anne went to the exclusive Rangi Ruru girls college in Christchurch, before returning to the homestead for a lifetime as chief cook and bottle-washer. 'You just had to do things. It was life,' she says matter of factly and without a trace of regret that despite her education she was expected to fulfil a domestic role within the family.

A huge window above the sink was one of the busiest parts of the kitchen. People would come and yarn with Anne while she peeled potatoes. She had a pony that would put its head through the window to try to find a treat; it loved the scum off the jam.

In 1955 electricity came on and, for the first time, Anne could use a modern iron as she went about starching and pressing the heavy linen tablecloths and napkins.

'The kitchen was always the centre of the house. There was no point lighting a fire somewhere else. It was always warm in here, and we stayed in here to eat most of the time. When I was a child we would eat Sunday dinner in the dining room next door.

'I had to cook because we had to eat. You rushed around with two pots of spuds, a leg and a shoulder of mutton roasting, and found a vegetable to cook. If you had cauliflower, you had to have white sauce. If you had lamb, you made mint sauce.'

There was once a separate 'cook shop', where a cook would prepare all the meals for the farm workers. But it closed down in 1936, after union bosses threatened the cook would lose his pension if he wasn't paid more. So the family took over all the farm cooking. 'You didn't do anything else. With the shearers, you'd be going full time on cooking. It was chops and sausages for breakfast, then morning tea, then hot lunch, then afternoon tea and then a full dinner. At one stage they all wanted supper too.'

Anne's nephew Richard now farms Langley Dale and they are joint owners of the homestead. In 1999 they agreed to the formation of the Langley Dale Homestead Trust to ensure that the house that has served their family over so many generations continues on, well into the twenty-first century.

'Just cleaning the gutters and doing the plumbing is a lot of work. All the pipes are original and they're corroding. The wetback on the stove went a while ago, so it's affected our hot water supply,' says Anne.

It's a grand old home, and while the trust will be working hard to ensure it remains so, Anne's workload is easing. These days she's not cooking and cleaning through the day and into the evening, and even has time for a hobby. 'I often work here in the evening at the table studying genealogy.'

Janet *I like English pub food like hotpots and winter vegetables*
de Wagt

A mouthwatering chocolate éclair perched temptingly on a pretty cake rack is just one of the treats awaiting visitors to Janet de Wagt's Dunedin home. But look a little closer and you'll find the éclair, the muffins and the fruit, indeed just about everything in the house, is plastic. Janet, a professional artist and community arts worker, lives alone amid the smooth and shiny splendour of one of the world's most extensive collections of plastic. 'Isn't it sad?' she jokes, looking around proudly at her plastic, mostly domestic ware and toys.

Janet has 21,000 pieces, most in storage, some housed at the Otago museum and a few thousand pieces throughout the house, including in her small and highly impractical kitchen. 'I can't even fully open the oven because it hits the wall. So when I cook in it, I just more or less throw things in.

'I eat out a lot. I like everything. I have expensive taste in food. I like fish and chicken, and a bit of red meat every two weeks.

'I do cook for myself. I have busy days. Sometimes I have been out there in the freezing cold working and I need a good feed. I like English pub food like hotpots and winter vegetables. I eat lettuces like other people eat apples.'

Kitchen renovations are on the drawing board for the new millennium, but Janet doubts it will help much on the cooking front. 'When I replace the kitchen, I know my head will say to make it better for cooking, but I won't really. I want to use all the space I can for the plastic. What you see here is a tiny amount of what I have.'

And what you do see in the bright green and cream kitchen are mostly reminders of past eras, from the green and cream canisters that set the colour scheme, to a much loved 1960s souvenir tray of the Royal Family, through to a Minnie Mouse lunch box. The floor, a decoupage made of a magazine of the Queen's coronation, completes the tableau.

It's a happy, colourful, cluttered space, but little of her precious plasticware is used day to day. 'The only things I use are the plastic jug, and my plastic glasses. Plastic is nice to drink from, it's not like years ago when there were sharp edges on it. I've always thought my plasticware is too nice to use. The sun knackers plastic and I prefer not to have a sunny kitchen because of that.

'I enjoy the social history associated with the kitchenware,' she says setting out a set of three Greggs jelly moulds, still with their original box. 'There are numbers on top of the jelly moulds and that shows that these are from the time when children started to have fun learning numbers.'

When she moved back to New Zealand after several years in England, Janet had accumulated 52 tea-chests of plasticware. She says all she really needs now is a big shed to store it in.

Oh, and maybe a garage. 'Did I tell you I have a collection of cars too?' she asks innocently but with a mischievous glint in her eyes.

Joan
I can't have the oven and the two hobs on or it overloads
Diamond

Joan Diamond's ageless, beautifully manicured hands speak of a life and times far removed from the Orewa caravan park she now calls home. For more than 25 years Joan lived in Rhodesia, now Zimbabwe. Cooking and cleaning were, by and large, not part of the expat lifestyle.

Post-independence Zimbabwe held little charm for Joan, but the move back to New Zealand meant losing a lifetime's savings through a pitiful exchange rate and moving down-market back in Godzone.

Still, she's quick to point out that she's invested her $18,000 wisely. 'This is what we call the Remuera of the camp. It's more expensive and better kept. At the other end, the quality of the people is pretty poor with druggies, boozers, and even a cross-dresser, although he doesn't know I've worked that one out!'

Joan's caravan is comfortable but predictably short on space. If she really wanted breakfast in bed, she could almost get it for herself without putting a toe on the floor.

'Despite the problems and its limits, I'll never have a house again. I hate housework and I can do it all here in half an hour. I don't have a vacuum cleaner, the Dustbuster is big enough.'

While the small size sometimes works in Joan's favour, it also presents continual frustrations. 'There is very limited power. I can't have the oven and the two hobs on or it overloads. So I can only cook in one pot and I don't find that very satisfactory.

'I cook very simple things, I was brought up by my mother to be a sensible cook. She lived on lots of grains and things, and she and my father only died relatively recently, at ninety-eight and ninety-four. They never ate fried foods and nor did we. I had five siblings and none of us liked eating out. We always wanted Mum's home cooking and I wouldn't go out to a restaurant even now. My bloke is English; he likes plain food too. We have meat and vegetables for dinner. Sometimes we have puddings, but not often because we don't have the money.

'Mum spent her life in the kitchen, hours and hours of time. She would sometimes serve up five different desserts at the one meal. I became determined not to do that because I remember thinking I would rather Mum had spent more time with us and less time on the puddings.'

Joan has mostly positive memories of her childhood and mixed reflections on her 25 years in Africa. She's kept a lot of mementos, and some of them decorate the kitchen-cum-living area. Those immaculate hands reach for a gilt-edged card as she shares one of the good times.

Joan once complained to the British High Commissioner on a first, casual meeting that her British partner didn't get invited to British functions, in contrast to her frequent invitations from the New Zealand High Commission. 'Well, this invitation was hand delivered and we went to their party. Everyone was dripping in diamonds and dressed up, and even though they had met us more than two months earlier, the High Commissioner and his wife remembered our names!' she chuckles.

Hinemoa Elder

This is currently our bathroom, kitchen and bedroom!

Hinemoa Elder isn't sure she'd recommend living among major kitchen and bathroom alterations. 'It's character building,' she laughs, then adds, 'or soul-destroying!'

When she moved from a grand old Remuera residence to a pretty ordinary house on Waiheke Island, with extraordinary views, trees and sun, Hinemoa knew there was a bit of work to be done. The kitchen was top priority, and has now been moved down a level.

'The existing kitchen is quite dinky, but it's not very family-friendly. With more than one person, it's a squash,' she says, standing in the original kitchen, which is tucked into the corner of the living room. The colourful paint job can't hide the tired joinery and both the fridge and the oven have seen better days. 'This is currently our bathroom, kitchen and bedroom!' she laughs, pointing to toothbrushes lined up on the windowsill above the kitchen sink.

Work on the new kitchen a floor below occasionally drowns out conversation. The job is nearly finished. 'I have never done anything like this before and I've loved it. I've gone round all the shops and suppliers and worked out what I wanted. Sometimes I've made up my mind and then looked at the price and said, "What?" and then found a creative alternative I could afford. And I've done some of the work myself. For example,

I sealed the concrete bench. Why get someone else in when you can do it yourself?'

Hinemoa designed the kitchen herself. The first things she ordered were concrete benches 1 metre high, instead of the usual 900 millimetres. She's tall and was sick of having to bend to chop and cook. She also wanted open shelving, good visibility and a simple structure that even children Millie and Reuben would find user-friendly. 'I was sick of the kids saying "where's this, where's that?" You have to believe kids suffer from a blindness the way they choose not to see things. If I have everything visible, the theory is they will just find things.

'It's a galley with an island but two separate working spaces. I wanted a cooker and a sink looking out into the room. There's nothing worse than cooking a meal and missing out on the fun. It's all about hospitality, having people over and food — it's a great combination and I hate to miss out because I am cooking.'

Hinemoa, a recently graduated doctor, is health conscious both for herself and the children. 'My kids like raw vegetables, which is very lucky. We have fresh produce, lightly cooked. Things like fresh fish, steamed or baked or poached, with herbs. It has to have taste and texture. The children really like pasta, rice and chicken dishes too. They will eat just about all adult foods now, like olives, artichokes and sushi. I often make sushi for their school lunches.'

While it's a family-friendly home and kitchen in the making, Hinemoa has opted to separate facilities for visitors. 'I have bought a caravan as a guest bedroom. It has cooking facilities. For Christmas, my father gave me a fitting that allows you to hook the caravan to the house, and his last present was a multimeter to check the current. The caravan has a little fridge, sink and cooker; it's self-contained; people can make tea and toast.'

Hinemoa's father came to stay recently and was impressed with the butler's sink, which Hinemoa had chosen. 'Dad reminded me that the house I grew up in, in Manchester, had a butler's sink. I suppose I have called on a lot of memories from my childhood in doing this.'

Milda Emza

I feel it is better to make it myself rather than buying it

Until she moved to New Zealand two years ago, Indonesian Milda Emza had never cooked a meal in her life. In fact, she happily concedes she'd never even made her own bed. 'I was brought up in a household where we had servants. It's not unusual in Jakarta to have maybe two or three household servants and a driver.'

All that changed for Milda when she married Tim, a New Zealander, and moved to New Zealand. The arrival of baby Miranda has also forced Milda into the kitchen of their tiny, modern Wellington apartment.

When asked if she likes her minimalist, stainless steel kitchen, she's a little bemused. 'I have never had a kitchen before so I don't know any different. I do like it, I suppose.

'When I first came here, I thought I could just go to Thai and Malay restaurants. But the food never tasted the way my mother made it. She is a great cook. She cooked for us with help from the servants. Mum is the best cook I have known from Sumatra. She was brought up in a small village where no one ever let you see them cook because they wanted to keep their cooking secrets. So my mother learned how to cook by peeping through her auntie's window!'

When she started cooking, Milda tried to follow some of her mother's recipes, but it wasn't that straightforward. 'When I tried to follow recipes, I didn't even know what some ingredients looked like when I went to buy them. So I asked my Indonesian friend here to help, and I looked some of it up in dictionaries.

'My husband says my cooking tastes like my mother's food, so I am happy. I feel it is better to make it myself rather than buying it and being disappointed about paying lots of money for food that isn't so tasty.'

Back in Indonesia, Milda used to be the presenter of a women's television lifestyle programme, but was happily relieved of the cooking segment after a less than credible performance. 'The women involved in making the programme said, "Milda, you look so dumb in the kitchen, we will get someone else to do that part of it!" And now my sisters hear that I am cooking, they can't believe it. They don't cook either.'

Now she's found her way round the kitchen, Milda is considering expanding her repertoire. 'I have an English cookbook called *The Confident Cook,* but I haven't started on it yet. I am not used to using an oven or ingredients like olive oil. I don't know what that would be like, but I would love to try.'

Laetitia Ferguson

I bring food in, and friends and family bring food too

When school groups visit Butler House at Mangonui, they often head straight for the kitchen. 'Even Sixth Formers, who you'd think would've been camping at least, can't believe you can have a kitchen where you can make a meal without pressing a button or flicking a switch,' says Laetitia Ferguson, who has lived on the Butler Point estate since 1972.

These days Laetitia and husband Lindo live in a new, bigger house on the same property, but the original 1840s cottage is tended with love and pride. 'We camped here while the new house was being built. It's always been lived in and we don't leave it empty for too long. We come down and stay here sometimes to keep the house company and light the fire to keep it warm. I am sure the house enjoys our visits as much as we do. I bring food in, and friends and family bring food too. There would always be someone staying in the house at those sorts of times. Mostly they're our overflows from the main house, but some family members prefer staying here.

'We've had reunions, two family weddings and many Christmas dinners here.

We either sit here in the kitchen at Christmas time or in the dining room next door. At any one time we've had about ten people for dinner here.'

An old, black wood-burning stove dominates the kitchen. 'It's on loan from the Otago Early Settlers Museum. It could be lit, but we don't because of the risk of fire. In the early days we think the Butlers probably had an outside kitchen or cooking area. They couldn't risk the fire burning the whole house down either.'

The old wooden table was originally a shearers' or butchers' table, according to Laetitia. 'We're not precious about it. It's well used — it has certainly been ironed on, you can see the mark from one of the heavy old irons they used to use. Another original item is the pine plate rack, which is about a hundred and fifty years old.'

A striking turn of the century sideboard displays china and other ornaments associated with the house. Laetitia laughs as she recounts telling a visitor of the painstaking task of stripping it back to the original wood. 'I told this American visitor that the sideboard had been painted seven different colours in the 1920s and that we'd had to work hard to get all that paint off. It turned out she was an expert in paint, and was horrified we'd removed it. She claimed the paintwork would have been as significant as the wood underneath.'

One of the frustrations of an old house is keeping it clean, and Laetitia says Butler House is no exception. 'No matter how long you spend on the brass, it never sparkles. It wouldn't matter how many maids you had, I can't believe it sparkled all those years ago either. The kitchen walls never gleam, but in the old days they would have been whitewashed more frequently.' She also concedes to a running battle with spiders, whose handiwork is evident in many corners.

The kitchen is well equipped with old kitchen implements, some of which came with the house and others that have been bought by Lindo. 'My husband finds all these things. I drive past the antique shops as fast as I can, but he can't let a chance go by!'

Beryl *I'm an old-fashioned English cook*
Gadsby

Christmas Eve is the highlight of Beryl Gadsby's year. She spends about two months, on and off, preparing food to make sure it's a special night for her family. 'My family have grown up expecting Christmas Eve to be done a certain way and it wouldn't be Christmas without it. I feel I have to carry on.'

Beryl and husband David immigrated to New Zealand from Derbyshire nearly 40 years ago with their children, Jonathan and Sharon. They loved New Zealand from the start, but Beryl determined early on that her family would grow up with her beloved English country food.

Now living in Takamatua on Banks Peninsula, in a transformed 1970s bach, Beryl says cooking has always been part of her life. 'From school age I took it for granted I would cook and do what my mother did. I am an old-fashioned English cook. I don't do fancy foods. I don't do Thai, for example, but I like going out to eat it. I cook things like Yorkshire puddings, Eccles cakes, pork pies and other English foods.

'Once I found sources of supply it was all easy enough. I had to find things like plain bacon instead of smoked bacon, lard instead of butter for pastry. People frown on lard these days and it wasn't always easy to find. I still make pastry and most of the time I find the lard, but I have had to have it rendered down at the butcher's sometimes. But you can't use butter; the lard makes the pastry shorter.

'It's English farmhouse fare — those raised pies are farmhouse food. They're what people look forward to on Christmas Eve. My children's friends come and they ask for the pork pies. One of their friends, who was born in England, has made me promise I will teach my kids how to make them before I pass on!'

The long preparation for Christmas Eve is offset with good-humoured inter-family rivalry, with a bake-off between Beryl and Sharon, and New Zealand-born daughter Tanya, to see who can make the best meat and potato pie.

Beryl is the first to admit that some traditional Christmas food isn't exactly suited to New Zealand's climate. 'Christmas pudding is a bit silly when it's so hot, with the shillings and all. I use five-cent pieces now. But the kids love it and the little ones love picking the coins out of the puddings.'

The countdown to Christmas starts in early November. 'That's when I make the Christmas cake and the puddings, otherwise they don't have time to improve. You need to keep a Christmas cake for a month to let the flavour spread through it. I make shortcake and put it in tins and give it to the family so they have things to offer people. I make four or five dozen fruit mince pies. I put them in tins and they keep for ages. But they certainly don't last long enough to freeze! I make a chocolate log as the children don't seem so fond of the traditional fruit cake these days. And I make little gingerbread men and houses, and they can go on the tree. On Christmas Eve I make trifle and fruit salad and then on Christmas Day I hand over to Sharon.

'I love cooking and I like to see the look on their faces when they see everything is the same as every other Christmas. They always look forward to coming home and I can't imagine Christmas without it.'

Christina *It's a clean and healthy way of cooking*
Gardiner

The thermal wonders that draw hundreds of thousands of gaping tourists to Rotorua each year are nature's kitchen to about a hundred local Maori, including Christina Gardiner. Twenty families live in steamy, watery Whakarewarewa Village, among them Christina, her husband, their son, daughter-in-law and 2-year-old grandchild.

Christina says the pools and steam boxes are part of daily life. 'It's a clean and healthy way of cooking. Most of the people in the village cook in the pools. If you put mutton into muslin and then into a steam box, the fat melts away and you can finish off the mutton, brown it off in the oven. It's tastier. It's the best way to cook silverside, it won't get dry or stringy.

'Vegetables cooked in the pool have their flavours enhanced, all the vitamins and minerals come to the fore. The pool contains minerals; this water comes from the core of the earth. People have been cooking like this since 1300.

'Tourists are stunned. They say, "Don't you suffer from sulphuric poisoning?" but when you're young you learn which pools to use for cooking. It's like a child

licking a spoon — when they make their own mixes and it doesn't taste right, they know. If the old people haven't cooked in the pools, you don't cook in them. You pass on your knowledge from one generation to the next.'

When Christina's grandchildren come to visit, she makes what the villagers call 'prepacks' to simplify the catering. 'We take a strip of tinfoil about the length of your arm, and place on it a piece of chicken, pork chop, potato, kumara, pumpkin plus stuffing. It's all raw and we fold it like a packed lunch. Then it gets put in a wire basket and into a steam box for an hour and a half. Each child is presented with a parcel. There are no dishes, no leftovers, it's a clean way of cooking and eating, and teaches the children to be tidy with food.' Tinfoil features a lot in steam box cooking and Christina says that because it's relatively cheap and easy to use, it has taken the place of tukohu, or flax baskets. Prepacks are also used for fundraising. 'Say the children are going to camp. Maybe two or three families will make prepacks and sell them for five dollars each. If they sell a hundred it saves parents having to pay out for the camp.'

The pools also make some money for the villagers. One of the highlights of any tourist's visit to the pools is a cob of sweet corn, freshly cooked in a hot pool, buttered and salted.

In addition to cooking, the pools provide hot water for just about every other household need. 'I don't possess a hot-water cylinder. Of the twenty households here, about ten have hot-water cylinders because of building regulations. We bathe in the hot pools and take what we need to wash dishes and clothes.'

As well as reducing costs and providing a healthy method of cooking, Christina says the pools also eliminate one of the worries that come with a conventional oven. 'When you are at the supermarket, you don't start worrying about whether you have left the oven on, if it's on high or low. With the food in the steam box or pool, you just don't worry.'

Da Vella Gore

Being an artist goes hand in hand with cooking

A trip to the Hokitika shops twenty years ago changed Da Vella Gore's life. 'I went to buy a pound of butter. I came home with a church instead! I saw them demolishing the church and told them to stop till I came back. I went to see the parish priest and bought the church on the spot.'

Since then, Da Vella, a professional artist and marriage celebrant, has spent two decades building herself a house and a chapel on her Lake Hayes property, made from materials from that church and four others.

Her simple, elegant kitchen has three main church influences. The arched doorways are an immediate giveaway, but the slate floor, once the roof of the Hokitika church, is a little less obvious. 'I was told I couldn't use the slate on the floor as it was too brittle and too thin. But it became my challenge to prove them wrong. I have set the slate into concrete to give it strength and made a pattern in the middle of it by setting a piece of old iron lace into the concrete and dropping tiles into the middle. The lines on the floor aren't exactly straight and it waves around a bit, but that's quite nice.'

The other feature reflecting the kitchen's origins is the marble bench top and servery. 'They're from the old altar. It's wonderful for making pastry!

'I adore cooking. It's another creative thing. Being an artist goes hand in hand with cooking, gardening, music and my art.

'I really enjoy Chinese food. Ben Ho, my artist friend, has taught me how to cook Chinese. It's not really hard as I keep all the ingredients here and the actual cooking time with Chinese food is quite short. Once you start with Chinese food, everything else seems so bland. I tend only to do a roast dinner when I have guests to share it with me. I live on my own so otherwise I wouldn't bother with that. But with a big roaring fire in the dining room, it's wonderful.'

The arched doorways and the windows are framed with curtains made of handmade Belgian Kunii lace, bought during a trip abroad. The cupboard doors are handmade copies of old church designs. 'I wanted to keep the Gothic theme. I didn't want to be able to see a dishwasher or microwave oven, so they're hidden behind doors. Anything modern looks wrong, but I had to have an oven and a fridge.'

Da Vella says that while she considers the house to be finished now, the church-buying bug won't go away. 'Just yesterday I went to The Warehouse to buy some glasses, and I also bought another church! You have to get your priorities right.'

Camille Guy

We eat really well here, probably better than at home

When Camille Guy says she takes everything but the kitchen sink when she goes camping, she really means it. 'I don't like grovelling on the ground when we're camping,' she explains, as she and husband Des unload their camp kitchen from a trailer to their campsite. The camp kitchen is a chipboard and plywood unit, with three levels of shelving and plenty of bench space.

Once the spacious tent is up, the kitchen is nestled into one side of the verandah, the gas double burner is put in position, and Camille's herbs, spices, crockery, glassware and utensils are arranged in their usual places.

One table, two chairs and a bottle of wine later, and life at the Tawharanui campsite is complete.

Camille is a foodie. She writes about food and nutrition and is currently completing a book about her concerns over the safety of soy. More than anything, she loves to cook, and she doesn't like to compromise much, despite a love of the great outdoors. After a few years of camping and making do, she and her brother designed and built the camp kitchen. It's been a godsend over the years, especially when Camille and Des's three children came camping with them. 'We put it on a trailer and once you're there it's worth the effort. Where we camp there are no facilities, so it gives a degree of comfort. In fact, we eat really well here, probably better than at home, because you can spend all day thinking about what's for dinner and there's no rush to cook it.'

While Camille's been able to replicate most of the home comforts, she concedes that camping still takes quite a bit of planning, especially as they have no fridge. 'We take a chilly bin, and we get ice every four days or so in Warkworth. We keep the chilly bin stocked up with milk, butter and yoghurt. We usually cook a chicken curry a week before we go and put it in the freezer. Then it goes into the chilly bin and we'll have that two or three days into our holiday.'

It's a challenge, she says, to see how long they can go without having to make the half-hour drive to Warkworth to get new supplies, and helpful fellow campers usually take turns bringing fresh ice and milk back for others.

Camille is mindful of food safety and most meals are vegetarian to eliminate the risk of food poisoning. 'Vegetables are easy because of the food hygiene thing. We take rice, pasta, and couscous, and a lot of prepared things. We like to be very comfortable so we have a lot of equipment and we take food and wine. You're roughing it anyway, so you want something that's a treat.'

Maree Hickey

I could quite happily have been a butcher

Maree Hickey teaches by day, caters by night, is a part-time sports masseuse, and fancies a job as a butcher. She's also a nun. Sister Maree Hickey, formerly known as Sister Patrick, or Patsy within the convent walls, is down-to-earth, talkative, and a very good cook. She joined the Sisters of St Joseph of Nazareth in 1962, at the tender age of 16.

Serving up a freshly baked apple shortcake, with cream and cinnamon yoghurt, Maree, one of nine children, says her cooking skills have been a great asset. 'Mum was the one who started me off with an interest in the kitchen. It was mainly a savoury start for me, learning to cook large quantities of meat. Living on the farm we killed a lot of that ourselves, both beef and mutton. The organs, livers, for example, were wonderful things to play around with, and sheep kidneys were superb. I could quite happily have been a butcher. Now I eat very little meat, but I still love dressing, it. We were great meat eaters.

'When I went to the novitiate in Wanganui we took a great quantity of meat, but a lot of the girls didn't know what to do with it. They hadn't dealt with large amounts of meat. I remember watching a magnificent piece of beef being cooked and shuddering, as they didn't know how to do it. When Mum gave a wonderfully prepared goose at Christmas time, some of the girls wouldn't believe what it was because of the long wing, they thought it was a leg!

'Everything was on a big scale. We had four Agas and a big Hobart food mixer, with big paddles for it. We had coppers to use for vegetable steaming and two big elements, which were brilliant; really good pikelets came off them.

'I went to Auckland once and did a course with General Foods. I heard about their courses for people who did catering on a large scale. There wasn't a great range of things, but I found it very helpful. They taught how to cook to scale, how to get the quantities right.

'It was all very silent at the novitiate, except during the holiday times. We had set recreation times, and outside that the rule of silence applied. Sometimes recreation was at meals. It was hard for me at the start, I couldn't see the point of it. I can remember vividly making little pies one day with another novice and I suggested we make little faces on each of them. So nineteen of them came out of the oven with all different faces, some happy, some crying, some with runny noses, and we were folded up, not laughing out loud, but still hysterical with laughter. The novice mistress came through, saw them, and I couldn't even speak to her, because I was scared of laughing. She made us turn them over and serve them so the faces couldn't be seen.'

In those days, Maree would be catering for up to 28 people a night. These days she lives alone in a house in the Wellington suburb of Newlands, and mostly cooks just for herself.

She also has a sideline in catering for private dinner parties. 'The bigger the catering the less likely a mishap. It can't go wrong, this home catering. You are working with the best of tucker, fillet of this or that. Ten is a breeze, but I can cater for eighteen to twenty.'

When she's finished teaching for the day, or put the finishing touches to dinner, Maree often relaxes with a glass in hand. 'I thrive on a good drink. I like a spirit or a good red wine.'

June Hillary

I do things like chocolate cakes, banana cakes, old-fashioned things

June Hillary's life is one of extremes. One day she can be trekking steep paths in the Nepalese mountains and eating pretty basic food, and a day or so later, among the great and the good at a black-tie Manhattan dinner. Wherever she is, June, Lady Hillary, is her own person despite marriage to one of the world's most famous men, and New Zealand's favourite son, Sir Edmund Hillary.

Their comfortable Remuera home, and the kitchen especially, are testament to their travels and rich life experiences. 'I am definitely acquisitive!' she says, looking at a shelved kitchen wall entirely devoted to family photos and pottery. 'I usually buy a bit of pottery wherever we go. We go away a bit,' she understates.

Several months of the year are spent on the road, either in Nepal and India doing hands-on work for the Himalayan Trust, or at fundraising dinners for the trust. Ed can easily draw a thousand people to a black-tie dinner at $500 a head.

'I don't mind all the dinners out. It's my job. I don't give the dinners or lunches.

In New York, where we had a large dinner with the Dalai Lama, we just swept in and it was all done. These days we often know people when we walk into the room. They all know who Ed is anyway. We just do the mixing and mingling.'

All the eating out does affect how June operates when she's enjoying time at home. 'We don't entertain much. When we are away, we are at fundraising dinners all the time so, no, we don't entertain. These days, if I have twenty-five people around I get caterers in. Sometimes it's up to fifty people.'

So, more often than not, June and Ed stick to a pretty simple regime. 'I am a plain cook. Ed likes plain things like casseroles and roasts. I don't do fancy things. I like things I can start at five o'clock so we can sit down at six o'clock to watch the news and have a drink. By then dinner is cooked and we eat at seven o'clock.

June also enjoys baking when there's a chance and points to a freshly baked sultana cake. 'It's at its best when it's hot, but it's terrifically indigestible! But it's a very good cake. I bake a lot but never stock the tins up anymore. I do things like chocolate cakes, banana cakes, old-fashioned things.'

Lured perhaps by the smell of fresh baking, Ed pops into the kitchen and puts a good word in for June's cooking. 'June cooks a very good cake. She's a good cook. I prefer simple meals like a good stew, potato, rice or roast lamb.'

Life has held its share of ups and downs for June, whose first husband, Peter Mulgrew, died in the Mount Erebus disaster. But she's not the sort of person to dwell on the negative, and relishes life. She has a simple recipe for keeping happy, foodwise, when she's on the road. 'I always take Earl Grey teabags and a packet of gingernuts with me wherever I go, and I ration myself to two gingernuts each morning. In India and Nepal we have tea in bed, it's divine!'

Ayolin
Ishac
If a man goes to the kitchen, we say he is a woman

It's a man's world in the Ishac household, even though they may never go near the kitchen. Ayolin Ishac, an Assyrian Iraqi, moved to Auckland with her husband in 1997 to be reunited with their family in the aftermath of the Iran–Iraq war. But she moved to Wellington in 1999 to look after her 37-year-old professional son. Her husband and two daughters remain in Auckland.

Ayolin's devotion to her son's needs is unremarkable among Iraqi women. 'My son can't cook or do housework. If he wants a glass of water, he says, "Mum, bring the water." I feel more comfortable with this even if I am sick.'

Sometimes Ayolin cooks her favourite dish, biriyani, for Iraqi and Filipino friends. It's also her son's favourite dish, but even so, he gets it only about once a month because of the enormous amount of preparation required. With her friends gathered round, Ayolin's small kitchen is crowded, with everyone offering help with the biriyani. It's a lively social gathering and various opinions are offered on the topic of men and food.

'Always in Iraq a wife does the cooking. The men do no cooking, no washing, no coffee, no tea, we make our own. Then at night, they want sex!' a friend comments, and the group erupts into gales of laughter. Another friend adds, 'If a man goes to the kitchen, we say he is a woman.'

It's not likely you'll come across many gender-confused men in these households if Ayolin is a measure of domestic duty. 'I spend all day cooking. I don't go out. If I don't cook, I knit. Sometimes I don't want to cook but I must and I must stay at home. But sometimes we go out and I will do some shopping.'

Ayolin manages well in her modest flat, but misses her kitchen back in Iraq. 'I had a very big kitchen. Our house was very big with many rooms. It was an Italian design, and in the kitchen there were three fridges, one freezer, a dishwasher, and a gas stove. I did all the cooking but when I went to work [she's a teacher] I had a cleaner.

'I like cooking, I learned it from my mother and at school. Not just Iraqi but also French and English cooking. I like all sorts of recipe books. I would like to make things off the television food programmes but they talk too fast and I cannot understand.

'Food is very important to us because we don't like to go out to picnics or restaurants. We like home food. When friends come round, we talk, everyone does something.'

Jillian
We eat seasonal food; I go with the flow
Jardine

A quick glance at the walls of Jillian Jardine's Central Otago kitchen gives you a pretty good idea of what might be on the menu for dinner. What started life as a humble bach used by shearers has been transformed into a warm, inviting farmhouse kitchen, with some idiosyncratic features. Among them are Jillian's favourite recipes, boldly scrawled on walls and cupboard doors. 'I started doing it when I needed glasses to look up things in my recipe books. I couldn't be bothered hunting through the books. And I would teach the children something simple to cook, like spaghetti bolognaise, adapting the recipes so they could understand the quantities and the like, and it seemed sensible to put them up on the walls too, so they could find and follow them easily,' Jillian explains. 'If you have adapted a recipe and want to use it a lot, you only have to look at the door or wall to remind yourself. I have fifty cookbooks — you'd think I didn't have time to look in them when you look at all this,' she laughs.

'I love cooking but seldom stick to recipes rigidly. We eat seasonal food; if it's winter it's hot things with winter vegetables. I go with the flow and use what is around. I grow as much as I can. We get a lot of free food too. Dick, my husband, goes out and comes home with ducks, goats, lamb, fish — and if he goes to the West Coast, we get oysters, scallops and crayfish. We do eat cheaply. Herbs are the most important things in my garden. I always use mint, rosemary, coriander, basil and parsley. I think that is very basic for any cook.

'We get ten people around the table. But these days it's often just Dick and me. We haven't had a family muster for a long time; the kids are really spread out.'

As the family has spread out over the years, so too has the kitchen. Jillian says the present kitchen was once the entire bach. 'We just knocked out walls till I got the size of kitchen I was after. I would build another kitchen just the same. The low ceiling makes it easy to heat in our climate,' she says, indicating a log burner that keeps the Central Otago winter cold at bay.

A long island bench in the middle of the kitchen houses many copper dishes and pots. A heavy wrought-iron utensil rack hangs from the ceiling, along with a number of baskets used to store onions and potatoes. The Welsh dresser displays mixing bowls of all different shapes and sizes, and brightly coloured plates from Greece decorate one wall.

Turkish saddlebags are draped over the backs of the two benches that flank the long dining table. 'We went to Turkey during the Gulf War. Everything was very cheap and we bought them and the floor rugs in bulk and freighted them back to New Zealand. We have never really spent money on the house, because we always say we're not staying here. That's what we say, anyway,' she laughs.

There are 12,000 sheep and 600 cattle on his 'hobby farm', as Dick jokingly calls it. With mountains forming a majestic backdrop and no sign of neighbours, it's easy to get the impression that Dick and Jillian are in some ways cut off from the rest of the world. The mere suggestion makes Jillian laugh. 'It's only fifteen minutes to Queenstown. We have all the illusions of isolation, but it's really not so.'

Sue Kedgley

On Saturday nights we always have organic pizza, which is delicious

Safe foods campaigner Sue Kedgley is inspecting one of the many lemons piled in bowls and baskets in her Wellington kitchen. 'There.' She smiles happily, pointing to the pitted skin. 'Blemishes like this are the seal of approval as far as I'm concerned. It means no chemicals have been on them and they always taste better for it.'

Sue lives in Wellington's Oriental Bay, with partner Dennis and son Zak. Elected to Parliament in 1999, she's a well-known feminist writer. Despite this reputation, she jokes that 'deep down maybe I am a deeply traditional woman!' when describing her ideal kitchen. It would have a large table in the middle where people would sit, talking and drinking, while she cooked. It's an unlikely scenario in her current kitchen which, while full of charm and character, is only just big enough for the family of three to eat breakfast in. 'We always eat at the dining room table at night. It's too small in here. If

I could start all over again with the place, the kitchen would not be in this spot, it's not sunny enough.'

A skylight directs all available sun into the small kitchen, which is full of brightly painted plates, baskets and other knick-knacks from various trips abroad. The Shacklock Orion stove is the only original item in the turn-of-the-century house, but it no longer works. Sue is contemplating replacing it with a wood-burner that would heat the whole house. But she wouldn't dream of a complete kitchen makeover. 'To me, most modern kitchens look like operating theatres. They're all white and sterile.'

Sue's preoccupation these days is the quality of food. 'People always think it's going to be too hard to ensure their foods are safe. But you learn how to read labels and always buy things as fresh as possible. Once you've worked out which products are safe, you just keep going back to them, so you're not always checking labels.'

She says having a healthy, safe-food diet doesn't mean doing it the hard way. 'There's a huge increase in fresh, ready-made food. People want good, convenient food, but it must also be nutritious. On Saturday nights we always have organic pizza, which is delicious.'

Most nights cooking is shared between Sue and Dennis. 'I am the kitchen-hand, and Dennis is the cook. I do all the shopping and get food ready to cook. If people are coming to dinner it's Dennis who titivates the food. He is naturally a good cook, and I am not.'

Robyn Kingston

I like the pigs because they are intelligent and a satisfying shape

Robyn Kingston's day starts as romantically as any of her 50-plus novels. Husband Don brings her breakfast in bed each morning, much to her delight. 'Don is a very good househusband,' she laughs, adding, 'they are hard to find.'

The hard-to-find husband is a common feature of Mills and Boon stories, and Robyn is one of their most successful writers. That has brought money and recognition but, most importantly, it has provided the means to the house of their dreams.

When they built in Kerikeri eight years ago, the architect's brief included the footnote that it needn't be a child-friendly zone as all their children had left home already. One result is a remarkable water feature running the length of the hallway. Water cascades loudly onto boulders and the resulting noise can be heard throughout the house. Robyn, who wears a hearing aid, describes it as a 'lovely white noise' that can be heard even when she's in the kitchen.

She otherwise prefers a quiet environment, especially in the kitchen. It's pale peach and fuss-free, exactly what she wanted. 'It's deliberately neutral because from my kitchen window I look out at our beautiful garden,' says Robyn, pointing to her lush green semi-tropical garden.

'I got a wonderful pull-out pantry installed, like a filing cabinet; you can see in both sides and right to the back. I decided on that when I just kept buying spices because I thought I was out of them, and then found I had five jars of paprika.'

A higher-than-usual upstand separates the kitchen from the dining room, and the top of Robyn's head can barely be seen when she's cooking. 'I am an exceptionally messy cook and wanted people to be able to talk to me while I cooked without seeing me or the mess!' Robyn explains. 'We eat quite simple food really. Don had a heart attack a few years ago so I've eliminated a lot of things from our diet.'

One of Robyn's private passions, her pig collection, is dotted round the kitchen. 'On a trip to Santorini in 1984, there was a lovely olive-skinned young man with pale eyes and he sold me my first pig. I have this thing about that sort of man; most of the men in my books are olive-skinned with those lovely piercing pale eyes,' she says, looking teasingly across to Don, who just happens to fit the description exactly. 'Now I find I have collected as many pigs as I have books, about fifty-five. I like the pigs because they are intelligent and a satisfying shape. Round with curves!

'As much as I like pigs, I do eat pork and bacon. I grew up on a farm and you eat anything really. I think that if you kill something you are honour-bound to eat it. I eat rabbit and hare; Don goes out and shoots them and I cook them. But I draw the line at songbirds — I would never eat them.'

Pat Lee

I thought Graeme Kerr was great, sloshing the wine in

'**I love pasta.** You don't have to peel it!' chuckles Lower Hutt mother of fifteen, Pat Lee. Pat and husband Don are parents of nine sons and six daughters, now aged between forty and nineteen. Due to the age span, Pat reckons there were 'only' thirteen children living at home at any one time.

Pat, now in her early sixties, says the family would munch its way through at least 60 kilograms of potatoes a month, as well as hundreds of sausages and mountains of mince. 'There was never enough, but you managed. I could make one chicken do for all of us, but there would be a lot of rice and it was pretty much "hunt the chicken!" You could always stretch a meal and make do with a little less. There was often an extra child or two and my mother had always made people welcome at the table, so I did too.'

Preparing breakfast, school lunches and dinner took up about six hours a day, but Pat says as the family grew so did her confidence and experience. 'With the first two children, I was always wondering if I was doing it right, but after that I didn't have time to think about it. I wasn't interested in anything except filling them up. I had help on and off, but not regularly. The kids had jobs, but you can't expect a twelve-year-old to cook for twelve people, can you?'

And common sense has ruled the Lee household in relation to special occasions. 'The children only ever had one birthday party, usually when they were five and there'd be something like pavlova. For their other birthdays, they could have two friends over and we would all have dinner together.'

Budget and ease of preparation were influences on Pat's cooking style, but so too were some of New Zealand's most famous cooking names. 'I thought Graeme Kerr was great, sloshing the wine in! He encouraged me to be adventurous in the kitchen. Alison Holst is great value too. And there's a bit of the Jo Seagar in me.'

Pat is a big fan of easily prepared foods like rice and pasta, which were not used in the average New Zealander's daily cooking repertoire until the last couple of decades.

While she enjoys good food, Pat says she is no fusspot. 'When I was in the home having the babies, it would amuse me that women would complain about the food. It was good, it was hot and there was heaps of it. All you had to do was sit down and eat it.'

These days, Pat says she loves her empty nest, although she sees a lot of her children and nineteen grandchildren. The kitchen was refurbished two years ago and she enjoys the extra storage space, view from the window above the sink and the clean navy and cream colour scheme. She's not sentimental about china or other kitchenware except for four little boy-and-girl salt and pepper shakers. 'They must be over sixty years old now. Probably not valuable, but they came from my aunt's boarding house where we stayed when I was little. There were eight pairs of them along a long table.'

The dining table at the Lee household is now down to two regulars, Pat and Don. Pat is still adjusting to cooking for just two, but says a son who flats down the road always looks after the leftovers.

She's still the chief cook, Don having no real interest in the kitchen. 'Cooking is a heart thing. It would be hard for me to cook for people I didn't care about. I couldn't cook for a living. If I don't care about the person's welfare, I can't cook for them.'

Sri Lloyd
I just put the fancy little lights on to make it look nicer

There aren't many student flats where crayfish, paua, mussels and scallops are piled high in the fridge and freezer. But this isn't just any old flat — it's 301 Willis Street, Wellington, a place with a legendary past and a catholic mix of inhabitants. The large two-storey house was originally designed and built as the German embassy, as the twentieth century began. Since then, it's been a brothel, reputedly the clandestine headquarters of the Communist Party, and, more recently, a student flat.

Time and student lifestyles have taken their toll on the once-gracious building. The kitchen, arguably, has fared the worst. Naked light bulbs hang from cobwebbed cords. Dirty dishes are piled on the otherwise clean and tidy stainless steel bench. The painted plywood-on-boards floor is scuffed and scruffy.

Sri Lloyd is one of seven people currently sharing the flat, most of them students. Sri, a commercial diver and provider of seafood delights, says she got over trying to clean the kitchen after her first three years there. 'There is fifteen years of filth on everything. Last time it was painted it was done with water-based paint, so even if you attack it with Jif, you remove more paint than grime. I would like to be able to water blast everything and I would like to see it restored.

'It would be an awesome place if it was done up. I've thought about what I'd do if I owned it, such as making the kitchen four times the current size. And I would not have all these people living here with me!' she says, referring to her six flatmates.

'We got a new oven last year, as you can see,' she jokes, pointing at a grease-caked oven about thirty years old. 'The last one just about melted down it was so old and that's what the landlord's put in for us.'

Three faded prints of the Last Supper grace one wall, above a shelf groaning with each flatmate's preferred breakfast cereal, and spreads. The flat has a high turnover. Sri has seen at least twenty people, students and others, come and go. Generally, she says, everyone cooks for themselves.

'Fortunately we are surrounded by take-out places. I eat out a lot. A couple of people will sometimes cook together, but generally we fend for ourselves.

'We get lots of crayfish. We have had up to half a dozen of them crawling around the floor! And we always have supplies of fresh fish, and scallops in the freezer. We get meat from Rob's [a flatmate] father's farm.'

Sri's flat was famous for parties. But no longer. Sri happily enforces a 'no parties' rule in the lease. And she has little truck with alternative lifestylers. 'While I would rather not be described as in any way alternative, we do have a few filthy incense burning vegetarians here with their lentils and mung beans!' she says, grinning broadly.

Despite claiming she's over the cleaning phase, Sri returns to the subject with no prompting. 'Ideally, I would have a kitchen with industrial lino going half way up the walls as well as over the floor so you could just hose it out from time to time. But because it's a lost cause, I just put the little fancy lights on to make it look nicer.'

Chris Lynch

On my birthday I am having a whole bowl of broad beans!

Even the floor of Chris Lynch's eco-friendly house, at Parakanui, is edible. Chris and her partner Andrew Sutherlands and their three daughters thrive on a mostly organic diet — including the waxed clay floor! 'The baby picks at it sometimes and eats wee bits of it. But she's still alive. It's all edible,' says Chris, laughing.

They've dubbed their kitchen 'the bridge'. It's a low-ceilinged, galley kitchen tucked away in a corner of the main family area and entry is up two steps.

'I wanted a farmhouse kitchen but we didn't really have the room, given the design we wanted for the rest of the house. But it's a thin, totally practical space. If the two of us are working in the kitchen, it's very intimate.

'When Andrew said we should elevate the kitchen and have steps, I said no. We debated it for a while,' she says, adding that she now has no regrets about the elevation. 'I like the size of it, but you can't have lots of people. It's not a many-people kitchen. I shuffle the kids out and you are cut off from the family area. But one of my favourite things is the window and the views from it. People like doing the dishes in our kitchen.'

Andrew built the house, using ecological principles, and Chris says that kept costs down. 'The sink is the most expensive thing we put in, otherwise it was all recycled material. I doubt the kitchen cost more than five hundred dollars. All the shelves are recycled wood. There is heaps of storage. We were used to student flats and when we moved in, I had all these empty shelves — and now we have filled them up and all the cupboards too!'

The coal range is literally the engine room of the house. It has a wetback and provides both water and underfloor heating, as well as being used for cooking.

Chris says she prefers organic food, and they grow a lot of their own. What isn't grown is bought locally from organic suppliers. 'Over summer, we were in full production and I had a barter system with the organic shops. I would go to the supermarket and come out with only pasta and a bottle of wine. That's all we needed to buy.

'We get organic meat. If Andrew gets it, it's at an exorbitant price from the shops, but I get it from a home delivery service at a reasonable price. I grew out of vegetarianism when I was first pregnant. We eat a bit of everything.' The three girls are thriving on their organic diet, Chris says, but for her upcoming sixth birthday, Chi has asked for dahl for dinner and as a treat 'no salad, please'.

'And on my birthday I am having a whole bowl of broad beans!' Chi boasts, proving beyond doubt her health-food credentials.

A hand-held electric blender is Chris's most loved kitchen aid. 'I love my wand! It's great for soups, mayonnaise, that sort of thing. When the kids get nine out of nine for their spelling they get to choose a dessert and usually it's meringues. It's great for that.'

The Lynch-Sutherland family are warm hosts to visitors and friends. They recently catered for seventy people when a friend married on their rural property. Chris was relieved the food side of things went well. 'The kitchen didn't break down despite the numbers. But that might've been the organic lager. Maybe no one noticed!' she laughs.

Lauren Lysaght

There is more pleasure in doing the cooking than being cooked for

Having children led to Lauren Lysaght's decision to enjoy food and cooking as much as possible. 'When the children came, I estimated how many meals I would have to cook in my lifetime and thought I might as well make it as pleasurable as possible.

'I am orally fixated, and hedonistic,' Lauren laughs. 'There is more pleasure in doing the cooking than being cooked for. I enjoy the ritual of it. I don't like to cook under pressure and I don't like producing anything that is substandard. I like presenting meals like works of art.'

Lauren and her partner Janet Frost live and work in a converted factory. Their home is also a product of imagination and artistic flair. 'It was the Helios Belts, Novelties, and Leathergoods Factory, which sounds like a cover for a holistic S and M den!' Lauren grins. 'It looked nothing like this. There was eighty years of grime and dirt, and it was full of abandoned stock.'

The top floor is a studio and downstairs is the living area. A lot of the factory features have been retained or revamped to fit in with their lifestyle and needs. The kitchen is open-plan, with the original factory concrete flooring. A huge copper extractor fan hangs over the bench, featuring a matador and bull motif. It's vented to the outside by a pipe, clad with old olive oil cans. There's a leather chaise longue, and the walls are adorned with paintings, advertising and movie posters, and Kiwiana. Dinner guests, many of them fellow artists, have tagged the upstand with their drawings.

Cooking is very important to Lauren and so is her domestic environment. 'In our old villa the kitchen was at the back of the house and this is a reaction against that. Food and talking and living are all entwined. I am very much influenced by my Italian-Irish descent and cook mostly food from the northern Italian region or Tuscany.

'We have this idea of Italians cooking glamorous food, but I stayed in a village there last year and their cooking was awful. They couldn't afford the right ingredients, so I offered to cook and they loved my Italian cooking. They mostly used Dolmio sauce and dried pasta. But they were incredibly generous and the wine was exquisite.

'I like doing risotto, and gutsy soups like Tuscan bean soup. It's a two-day job. It's much better the day after it's first cooked. I make the bread to go with my dishes.

'I am not the definitive cook, though. And I don't trust people who don't eat. There is something missing from their make-up.'

Her impatience with non-eaters is matched by her disappointment on the rare occasions she eats out. 'We have virtually stopped going out for dinner at restaurants because I have become so critical. I can't stand the noise, you're treated like you're fit for the old age home if you want the music down so you can talk, and you pay to suffer rude waiters and cigarette smoke.'

However, she has nothing but rave reviews for her favourite cook, Marcella Hazan. 'She's a wonderful Italian cook. But I think you should treat cookbooks like sex manuals — read them once, put them away and then just use your imagination.'

Diane Marchant

The table is often dominated by school work, but we do eat there

Despite living in one of the most isolated parts of the Marlborough Sounds, Diane Marchant's pantry is full of exotic goodies. Diane, a former flight attendant, her pilot husband, Cliff, and their three children moved to a 200-acre property in the southeastern corner of Port Gore thirteen years ago. The oldest child, Karen, was only five at the time, and two more children have been born since.

Diane says family life became too busy to develop the fishing lodge they'd intended, so she and Cliff mostly have friends over on a casual basis. Most of the time, she is chief cook and bottle-washer for everyone.

Despite a desire for new interests, Diane doesn't have a lot of time on her hands. 'I have taught the children correspondence right up to seventh form and Karen has just gone off to polytech. Paul is doing seventh form, Nicky is in the fifth form, Christopher and Michael are Forms One and Two. I have the three older children doing their correspondence work in their rooms, and the two younger boys work at the kitchen table. It's a bit of a disaster as they have a lovely big view and they are easily distracted. The table is often dominated by school work, but we do eat there.'

A large room at the front of the house serves as combined lounge and dining room, and there's a separate kitchen. 'I have just done up the kitchen for the second time. It was built in the 1920s and in those days the walls were lined with newspapers. We found an article saying how amazing it would be if you could fly across the Tasman! Cliff cut it out and kept it because he has actually left here, gone to Wellington, flown to Sydney and back and come home all on the one day!' she laughs.

A huge servery between the kitchen and the dining area is Diane's saving grace, allowing her to cook, teach and play air-traffic controller, all at the same time. 'I can be cooking in the kitchen and, through the servery, teaching the boys at the same time. Or I am on the radio talking to Cliff. Sometimes if he is coming in on the 767 from Singapore to Christchurch, and is high over the West Coast, he can call me up.'

Cliff is away half the year on international flight duties, but he pulls his weight when it comes to domestic chores. 'As we run out of things, we write a list. I fax the list through to Soundsair; he picks it up and goes to the supermarket in Wellington.' Cliff then loads up their small plane and makes the quick hop across Cook Strait to home.

Cliff is an amazing shopper — when he goes away to Japan, for example, he will come home with little packets of ingredients because he has been out and had a neat meal and he wants to try it at home! He will bring packets with Japanese instructions and little pictures and you work out that it's probably a sauce that's meant to go on fish! I have a lot of things like that in the pantry.'

Diane's nearest neighbours are one and a quarter hours' drive away, along a very rough 15-kilometre stretch of road. It's a three and a half hour drive to Blenheim. But Diane says she's not lonely and even has occasional unexpected visitors. 'I was here on my own with the kids and two divers in wetsuits turned up in a boat. They had come round from Queen Charlotte because it was too windy. Cliff had phoned to say he couldn't get in with the friends he was bringing, so I had this huge meal and no one to feed. These guys were freezing and asked if they could use a barn, but I told them they could use the bunkhouse and I asked them to share our meal. It didn't go to waste!'

Tara Mathis

I prefer cooking sweet things because it's fun for me

The Mathis family of Upper Atiamuri could argue the merits of lemon icing till until cows come home. And with nearly 900 cows on their two dairy farms, that's some argument.

The icing on the cake or, more precisely, 14-year-old Tara's banana cakes, is the key to her fame not only within the family, but also among friends and some grateful Massey University students. Tara has been cooking since she was about five, although she explains: 'I didn't do great things then, but I helped quite a lot.'

From modest days of licking the bowl, which she admits probably attracted her most in those days, she's built up quite a repertoire and reputation as a cook. For the last few years, she's taken her turn cooking for the whole family maybe once or twice a week but, from a very tender age, she has chosen to specialise. 'I prefer cooking sweet things because it's fun for me, more so than making a whole meal. And people tend to enjoy eating sweet things. I get a better result with sweet things.'

For Christmas last year, Tara made gingerbread houses for her close friends. They were a labour of love, each taking a total of at least three hours. She says she likes things that require attention to detail and working out fiddly bits. And while her efforts go down a treat, Tara concedes her passion for cooking isn't shared by her sweet-toothed friends. 'They think I am nutty and it's a waste of time. When my friend Lucy came out here, she asked me what I was doing, she couldn't understand why I wanted to bake. I take it as a joke. I enjoy cooking, more than eating food. And my friends enjoy the eating part.'

So do her parents, Mary and Brian, and university student brothers, Karl and Adam. 'I make banana cake every weekend. Once the boys went to uni, I started sending cakes to them. I have couriered them sometimes. When they first went down to uni, they made a point of asking me to make sure they got their cakes. If neighbours are going past, they will take them for me, but if I am couriering them, I pack them in with honey biscuits with a cube of chocolate in the middle.'

Lemon icing is Tara's trademark, and her brother Karl offers unsolicited praise of her baking. 'The cakes are good! My flatmates like them as well. We can never have too much; it's the highlight of the week. But they only last a day, not a week.' And the lemon icing? 'Is there any other icing?' he teases, and the whole family gives a resounding cheer.

The whole Mathis family shares Tara's love of food, but her ability to cook has, it seems, almost completely bypassed her brothers. 'They are both hopeless! One can only do fry-ups. Mary went through a stage where we all cooked one night a week. Karl could only do steak, I would do something like fettucine, and Adam would do fried eggs, bacon, and onions. I have given up on him.'

Despite her flair in the kitchen, Tara is not planning a career around cooking and food, and is reserving her options for the future. But she says if she has children of her own some day, she'll make sure any sons as well as daughters know how to cook. She'll have a few other tips for them too. 'I would probably say the presentation is the most important thing. I try to make things look good.'

83

Mazz Maybury Freed
I have ultra-wholesome food, with very energetic vegetables

'**I love simple, fine food**, prepared with love and care. You can always taste that,' says Mazz Maybury Freed. Exotically dressed and made-up, Mazz lives in an old inner-city Auckland apartment she calls the Grotto. Virtually every space is covered in something sparkling and dozens of candles flicker, enhancing the Grotto's twinkling appearance.

Mazz's kitchen curios range from tiny perfume bottles stored in an old printer's block to a display of much-loved but rarely worn shoes. Her old ballet shoes hang from the ceiling, along with crystals, and when she's cooking, she's watched over by a large statue of the Virgin Mary and a variety of angels and cherubs. Her fridge is covered in children's drawings — she is fairy godmother to several of her friends' children.

Mazz says she loves food and loves cooking. 'I have been vegetarian since I was a child. I noticed then that meat made me feel sleepy and not like playing so I told my mother. I was about nine. She understood and was very supportive of my not eating meat any more. So now I have ultra-wholesome food, with very energetic vegetables! I love avocado and eat lots of salads.'

Mazz says she has lovely times in her kitchen, which she describes as nearly perfect. 'I have special things all around me. On the fridge is a photo of one of my grandmothers, who was a great cook. In fact, both my grandmothers and two great-aunts were great cooks and I loved being in their kitchens. I spend a lot of happy time here thinking about them while I cook.'

Mazz mostly cooks and eats alone. 'I am too busy working to cook for other people. Until recently, though, I always had company. I had a mannequin and she lived just by the kitchen door. She had a blissful face, was very quiet, never in a bad mood. In return she received unconditional love. But a friend recently moved to a fantastic apartment and she's decided to live there for a while.

'If I could change anything about this kitchen, I would love to have a view and a garden. I live in the city, serve the city, but have my heart in the country and a simple life in abundance.'

85

Wendy
We grow tropical guava, apples, ginger, sunflowers, wheat ...
Medicine-Isis

If you crossed Xena, Warrior Princess, with Alison Holst, you might just come up with Wendy Medicine-Isis. Wendy, who describes herself as a travelling magical fairy, shares a two-storey cottage with five others, including 4-year-old son Ocean, in the backblocks of the Bay of Islands.

From the outside, the cottage appears in need of some tender loving care. Once inside, however, the look is not so much cottage as earthy chic cave-dwelling. Home-made mosaic floors are gradually taking over where vinyl once dominated, strips of tree bark decorate the walls, along with Ocean's art, and home-grown fruit and vegetables are carefully stored.

Wearing a patchwork dress made especially for the now infamous Sweetwaters festival, where she sang and sold grass-based drinks, Wendy completes her outfit with a purple floral apron and a garland of silk rosebuds. 'I love to dress up, but with this lifestyle you ruin nice clothes. Most of the time I am mucking about in the mud and the garden and look like a labourer. So I dressed up specially today, you bet!'

The 24-year-old says that despite her love of the land and encyclopedic knowledge of plants and their uses, she was originally a city girl. 'I started getting into nature when I was seventeen, after two years of a fairly wild life on Queen Street. I started travelling around the South Island as a magical travelling fairy, which I'd wanted to be since I'd read about pagans while I was a child. I wanted to keep that sort of lifestyle going. I got pregnant at nineteen though, and ended up living in a house-truck and a shack. This is very comfortable living for me now. When it was a caravan it was much harder. I'm just lucky Ocean has been such a good boy.'

It was while she was travelling that Wendy adopted the name Medicine-Isis. 'Medicine' because she discovered that she was a medicine woman. And Isis was the Egyptian mother goddess of the earth, something that appealed to Wendy. She retained her given name, which was invented by J.M. Barrie for the Peter Pan stories, the magic of which is significant to her.

Wendy is grinding home-grown sunflower seeds to be made into a tapenade or to go into chapatis for a lunch being prepared collaboratively with Scooter and Clinton, two of her housemates. Just about everything that's needed for the three-course lunch is home-grown. 'Any foods we have to buy we aim to grow and we try growing everything. And for this we use only heirloom open-pollinated cuttings, so we are growing food from the seeds our grandparents would have used.'

She recites a long list of fruit, seeds, and other plants grown on the 1.2-hectare site. 'We grow tropical guava, apples, ginger, sunflowers, wheat, herbs, citrus, avocado, mangoes, feijoas, nuts, garlic, sprouts, pineapples, onions, pumpkins, potatoes, carrots, peaches, bananas, berries of all sorts, and even sugar cane, but that's not in production yet. We don't buy eggs or milk, we use soya milk, or make sunflower seed milk.' They also run a compost and worm farm, and Wendy makes home-brews of beer and wine.

Wendy concedes there are times when food supplies run a bit low. 'When we run out of food we eat dandelions, chickenweed, plantain, and sheep sorrel. They go into

salads and are pretty good. We cultivate yarrow, and use flowers. With nasturtiums you can use the flowers and the leaves. Violets are good too, and feijoa flowers are fantastic. We love wisteria flowers too.'

Wendy recently bought a washing machine, one of the few traditional home comforts she has. 'I love this life. Fancy electricity is a bit much, but when you are a parent it's different and you have to be more responsible. But sometimes we pretend not to have electricity and just enjoy candlelight and raw foods.

'My greatest luxury in the kitchen is the lights. I haven't had a good light to cook under for the last five years. The electricity runs the lights, the washing machine and

the stereo, that's all. We do all our dishes in cold water, don't use a sink and don't use chemicals to clean them. A wooden scrubbing brush does a good job.

'My biggest challenge in the kitchen is sharing it, because of the other couple who usually live here. You have to work in with people and cruise along, but when they're away we let the dishes stack up a bit longer.

'We altered the kitchen when we came, and took out some pretty awful shelves and things. We got a big totara post and put that in, and it supports the ceiling as well as the bench. The bench is a big slab we saw at a sawmill. We jumped in the ute, chain-sawed it, and towed it up here. We made Ocean his own little table at the end of the bench and he does things like juicing.' Ocean interrupts his mother to explain proudly that his table is 'solid as'.

'Everyone is always experimenting with food, either being fruitarian, or sproutarian, or we have dough days where we just eat bread things,' Wendy continues.

Despite the fact that she prepares virtually every ingredient for every meal from scratch, including milling wheat for flour, Wendy doubts she spends longer than many other cooks preparing meals. 'It would take me forty-five minutes to make chapatis, salad and steamed vegetables. Raw food doesn't take any time at all. Sometimes I will spend three or four hours baking, especially now Ocean is at kindergarten and needs biscuits and little cakes. I like baking: making muffins, bread, cakes and biscuits.

As well as being able to turn a few weeds and herbs into a nourishing meal, Wendy is also a dab hand with the sewing machine. 'We buy bags of rags for a dollar and make our clothes out of them. I would like to learn how to weave and I've just been learning pottery from a neighbour. It would be good to make carpets and bedspreads, rather than spending money on that sort of thing. I dye fabrics with plant dyes from our garden — wheatgrass, for example, gives an almost fluorescent green.'

For all its back-to-nature goodness, Wendy's lifestyle is demanding and disciplined. If she gives up gardening for a few days, the group's food supply is jeopardised. Despite that, she says there's no going back to more conventional home comforts. 'I couldn't go back to the city. It's not my heart's desire. But if I had to for some good reason I would. I had to live in Hamilton last year for four months, but I don't feel well when I am in treated houses full of plastic, with fridges going all the time. That constant hum gets to me.'

Kath Wendy
I come from a very conservative background

Wendy's mother, Kath Wendy (she changed her 'sur'name to what she calls a 'lady' name) lives two minutes' walk down the path from her daughter and grandson. A dreadlocked granny in her early forties, she lives in an old bus, and her partner lives in a hut on the same property.

They share a home-made kitchen they call Bellamy's Kapai Whare Kai. 'It actually started as an old canvas tent and we built around it until only the pole was left. We tore the canvas down and we had a kitchen. When we started we used old tyres and they form most of one of the side walls. But we got bored with the tyres and started to use other materials. We found the windows and just about everything else at the dump.

'It used to have better murals on the outside walls but they've faded and washed out. It did have a lovely goddess, but you can't really see her now. I am getting a big plastic tiki soon, from a friend, to go on the door.'

The flooring is shell and gravel, and Kath says it's wonderful. 'One of the best things about this place is that you don't have to worry about making a mess. If you drop something, the dogs eat it, and you throw peels away. My compost heap is out the window; I just throw scraps out and it all starts growing again. I am quite fussy about surfaces and keeping things clean, I don't like dishes piled up and clutter.

'The pantry is from an old bach at Piha, which was being demolished. It has made a big difference as we used to get rats and mice in the food.'

Kath's only mod cons are cold running water and two hotplates fuelled by a gas bottle. 'I would love an oven, like Wendy's, I miss making things like casseroles and scones. We eat well and cheaply. None of us starve. My great luxury is organic coffee, which is hellishly expensive. I have it with honey and soymilk. Coffee is the only thing that wakes me up — it's my only drug.

'If anyone runs out of food we just go down the road to someone else. But at this time of the year, I do get a bit sick of soup and dahls and I am looking forward to some raw foods and salads.'

Kath's off to a pagan party, and not sure what to take. But as she talks she grates carrots, yams and beetroot, throws in some leaves and flowers and the problem is solved with the creation of a tasty, colourful salad.

Despite being a hippie to the core, Kath says she spent a whole weekend organising the kitchen once it was built. 'I booted my partner and my younger daughter out so I could have everything done the way I wanted and within reach.

'I come from a very conservative background. My mother is part Fijian and I wonder if my strange ideas come from that part of my family. My mother can't figure out the way I live. She worries about me and thinks I am getting colds and living in poverty. I don't think it's such a bad thing to be a bit cold and uncomfortable.'

Rachel Miller

We have two commercial ovens, six large gas hobs and a hot grill

Rachel Miller happily admits she's sometimes lost in her own kitchen and hasn't a clue what's in the fridge. Kiwi-born Rachel is married to Australian diplomat Geoff Miller, and their latest and last posting is Wellington. Rachel's home, a large house with room to entertain up to a hundred guests, is in the diplomatic enclave of Khandallah.

The kitchen spreads over two or three rooms and is run jointly by Rachel and her chef, Alison Lyes. The two women work together harmoniously, but Alison always calls Rachel 'Mrs Miller', and a healthy professionalism pervades their down-to-earth approach to sharing the kitchen.

Official functions often dominate Rachel's schedule. When she's not out on the diplomatic circuit, she's often home entertaining or planning the next function. She says it requires a lot of planning and staff management. 'In addition to Alison, we can have up to six people and a kitchen assistant working behind the scenes for a dinner. We can cater for forty-five people sitting down and up to a hundred for a buffet.

Despite numbers that would daunt many, Rachel and Alison agree the official residence's kitchen works very well. 'The residence was built in the mid-1970s, still within the era when there was a flower room provided, a butler's area and a dumb waiter. Now, with cuts in funding, you wouldn't find residences being built with all those things. But they really are essential to running a place like this,' says Rachel. 'We have two commercial ovens, six large gas hobs and a hot grill.

'One of the things we've had to do here is install a southerly-proof extractor fan. Before it was put in, you'd open the front door and could smell exactly what was for dinner. The southerly just blew right into the kitchen through the fan.'

The two women point proudly to a pot storage system they devised jointly. 'We lack storage. So Alison and I designed pull-out pot storage under the centre table. I copied the idea from something I'd had when we lived in Seoul,' Rachel explains.

There is talk of redesigning the kitchen. Everything is scattered over five fridges, for example, in different parts of the kitchen. It's Alison's job to keep the kitchen in order, but with frequent use of casual staff, things are often moved from their correct place. With a better layout, she thinks her job would be easier.

But some challenges of catering en masse can't be avoided. 'It's a bit like a restaurant but, unlike a restaurant, we have to serve everyone at once. They just serve one table at a time. So we have to juggle things around,' says Alison.

Planning cocktail parties and dinners is a shared pleasure, both women agree. 'Alison and I can sit here all day looking at cookbooks. My favourites include *The Sugar Club Cookbook* and *The Paramount Cookbook*. I also love Beverley Sutherland Smith, *A Taste for All Seasons*, probably the first modern Australian cookbook. I also have my father's cookbook from the 1920s. It's called *The Gentle Art of Cooking*; it's well worn and well used. He liked to cook special things, and he would always do the main course for dinner parties. I also have my mother's cooking journal, which was made for her before her marriage.

'The ingredients here are very good. New Zealand seafood is so good, we will serve things like a light salad with scallops or oysters. Fish is excellent and things like asparagus, at three ninety-nine a kilo, are wonderful. And this is only the start of the season.'

Alison, who has worked in embassies, restaurants and chateaux all over the world, agrees that New Zealand's produce is a blessing. 'Everything in New Zealand is seasonal. It makes things so much more exciting to have.'

Rachel says that while the residence is partly a restaurant, first and foremost it is a home, albeit a diplomatic home. 'I find it quite odd because I am never sure what we have in the kitchen. I don't know what vegetables are here and can get quite lost at times. If I decide I want spaghetti sauce and there is no tomato paste, I have to head off and get it. In my own kitchen, I would always have that, but everyone has different staples.

'Sometimes at the weekends, Alison will leave us something, but at other times I cook. It's often comfort things, like lamb's fry, which Geoff loves, or spaghetti sauce. It's hard to get used to using a commercial stove for small amounts and the hobs are so powerful that I cook the rice on the pilot light!'

When Geoff and Rachel's term in Wellington comes to an end, they'll be retiring to a terrace house in north Sydney, Rachel's first chance to have a 'real' kitchen. 'I

want a workable kitchen, with a dining area. There is a dining room, but we will turn it into a kitchen and dining area. I think a small galley kitchen would be good, I have seen one in a magazine I like. I don't want to be stuck in the kitchen with everyone else having fun somewhere else. I want to be able to see people and talk to them as I cook. But I don't want them to help out,' she adds firmly.

Rachel says she wants to get up to speed quietly on her somewhat rusty cooking skills. 'What goes first is your timing, that ability to have everything ready at the one time. You just forget how to do it. And also the strength in your right arm. I'll have to build it up. If you are using your arm to mix something, you certainly feel it the next day. Pavlovas for example.'

Mention of pavlova inevitably provokes discussion of national food identity and ownership rights, a topic that Rachel has to confront continually throughout diplomatic life. 'I think this is one of the most difficult things. You're always asked things like "What is your traditional food?" or "Will you cook something for the bazaar?" What do you cook? Pavlova, obviously. No one outside of New Zealand and Australia cares who owns it.

'I tried to do lamingtons for a fair in New York. I ended up knee deep in cake crumbs, chocolate icing and coconut. I just couldn't do it. I got to Tokyo and we had a French-trained Japanese chef and he could make a million lamingtons with no fuss at all. They were stunning.

'We serve lamb, kangaroo, emu, possum even. But you can't find kangaroo readily outside Australia. We used to be able to buy it here, but it stopped coming into New Zealand.'

Rachel has fond memories of many successful dinners but says the most relaxed was not for diplomats or politicians, but for journalists. 'After the entrée, about four of them jumped up and I quickly figured out what they were up to. So we got ashtrays out and put them on the tables and after that it was a great fun dinner, the noise level was incredible.

'Small round tables work really well. A long table looks great with the flowers, the crystal and china, but people can get stuck. You have to try to dispense with protocol a bit so not all the diplomats are together with everyone else somewhere else. You can do that in some countries, but you wouldn't try it in Japan, for example, where everything is much more formal.'

Having been posted to Tokyo, Malaya, Indonesia, New York, New Delhi and Seoul before Wellington, Rachel says limited supplies and variety of food can be common. 'In Korea, during our time, you could only get carrots. You ate carrots, carrots, carrots. We would bring in cartons of Surprise peas for a bit of variety. Pineapples

cost two hundred dollars each and lemons one dollar each. People would buy them, cut them up and freeze them, so you could offer people a little bit of lemon with their gin and tonics!

'Having lived in Asia, I'm a big fan of Asian food. When my daughter and I are together we cook Japanese food, because there is a lot of preparation and cutting involved if you do it properly.'

Now, as Rachel prepares to pack up, she looks out the kitchen window and across Wellington Harbour, and says she'll miss one aspect of the kitchen in particular. 'This is the best view in Wellington. The view makes up for the blandness that comes from it being a commercial kitchen. The gardener is under instructions to keep the hedge trimmed so the view can always be seen.'

Margaret Northcroft

I cook things that take a very short time

When Margaret Northcroft heads towards the kitchen the last thing on her mind is cooking. Margaret, a Wellington photographer with a degree in science, renounced cooking nearly two decades ago.

'When my sons were eleven, thirteen and fifteen, I told them they would have to eat for the rest of their lives so they could take over the cooking. So they took turns, week about, with the cooking, the washing, and the marketing. They thought it was a great idea. They wanted alternate nights to start with, but I wasn't prepared to police it! My husband does the dishes.

'I didn't want to be involved in the kitchen at all. I am not keen on cooking. During those years they had to forward plan if they weren't going to be home the night it was their turn to cook. They never swapped with each other, they just made provision for not being there, like cooking double quantities and freezing some.'

Margaret's kitchen was designed and built in 1993 by one of those enthusiastic young cooks, Bernard, who trained as an architect. 'He made up a model and said, "If you don't want it, get someone else to do it. If it's okay, then leave it to me." I had no doubts about it. I just wanted no double-handling of things. I didn't want to take things from the dishwasher and have to pull open drawers and cupboards to put them away. I didn't want much walking around either and everything had to be easily to hand. There's no outstanding feature, because the whole thing is outstanding,' she says proudly.

Margaret says Bernard designed the kitchen for himself and his brothers; he argues it is simply a very practical cook's kitchen. Bernard's concept for the kitchen was to create 'an interesting collection of furniture for a dynamic kitchen'. Each piece has its own unique features and materials, and some even have the ability to move and change the whole look and feel of the kitchen. For example, a large wooden door that operates on a garage 'tilt a door' mechanism. When the door is open, whoever is cooking has the kitchen door directly over his head.

'They [the boys] are all six-foot plus, so the bench is higher than standard. It's perfect for tall people, but everything was designed to be in easy reach for me,' Margaret says.

The small kitchen has an industrial look — a cross between a science lab and a restaurant kitchen. Bernard attended to every last detail, including the manufacture of an 'icebox' as the eerily glowing fridge is called. The 'icebox' is, in fact, a large Fisher and Paykel fridge. Bernard spent two months building a frosted Perspex and polished aluminum casing around it, with fluorescent lights sandwiched between the two.

A fruit tree stands like a large coat rack, made from a wooden pole, wok sieves, hose clamps and materials found throughout the rest of the house.

There's no rangehood — instead, a powerful industrial extractor fan was adapted for domestic use. To say it's highly effective is an understatement, it seems. 'When it's steamy the steam and the food fly out the window!' Margaret jokes.

Meat hooks, arranged above the stainless steel bench, hold dozens of stainless steel cooking utensils. 'I had a friend come to look at the kitchen and she said, "Look at all the meathooks and you're all vegetarian!"'

Given her lifelong antipathy towards cooking, Margaret was sad when the boys started to leave home and she now reluctantly takes turns with the one remaining son. 'I cook things that take a very short time. Salads are good; couscous is even faster.'

Years ago, when the family lived overseas, Margaret played her part as a dutiful social hostess, but says those experiences did nothing to convince her that it was worth persevering with. 'We once had a barbecue. I timed the whole process. It took four hours to set up and then four hours to demolish and I had a miserable time.' But in those days the option of using commercial caterers was frowned on as an abdication of domestic duty and so entertaining was just gradually scaled down and virtually phased out.

'I find the whole thing of people having you over and you having to have them back just ghastly. Luckily, it's stopped in our street. My neighbour, who is a great cook, has seen my repeated efforts at light-as-air chocolate sponge cake. I produced four discs and then a puny looking thing. She couldn't believe it.'

Little, it seems, can lure Margaret into the kitchen. She's even given up making tea and coffee.

But she lights up as she opens the freezer section of the icebox and pulls out two birds. There's no chance, however, that the birds will end up on the dinner table. Both are carefully preserved in plastic bags and in almost perfect condition — one a red-billed gull and the other a kingfisher. Margaret always keeps a plastic bag in her car on the off chance she'll spot dead birds worth salvaging.

As she admires her most recent finds, she says husband Roger recently commented he thought they'd had something similar in a freezer a long time ago. 'I said yes, it was an albatross. It was from the Wahine storm.'

By law, the kingfisher, a protected species, must be offered to Te Papa, but the red billed gull may have a different fate. Margaret keeps a magpie skull with bill intact in the living room. 'I just like them. Henry Moore always had this sort of thing. Both my parents were artists so it may be a combination of art and science.'

Marian
I like things I can make with my hands
Abukar Osman

Camel's milk is just one of the things the Abukar family misses about life in Somalia. The milk, and camel's meat, were part of their daily diet, but after more than five years here they've adjusted to New Zealand life and worked out ways of ensuring most other aspects of their traditional cuisine survive.

Their spotless council flat in the Wellington suburb of Newtown betrays little evidence of its eleven inhabitants: parents Marian and Mohamed, and their nine children, who range in age from 21 down to 1 year.

Mohamed and daughter Zahra interpret for Marian as she explains their special needs as Somalians living in New Zealand. 'We are Muslim and need halal food. We never have pork or ham. A lot of people say halal is not available but we have learned where to go. Before that we only ate fish and vegetables because we must have halal. It took a long time to find out everything and to know what is good for us to eat here.'

The family rarely, if ever, eats out because of their concern about halal food. 'We are always worried about it. So we prefer to eat here. People will tell you food is halal but you don't know.'

The family observes Ramadan and the children are given an early introduction to fasting. 'The children start to learn to fast at about seven or eight years of age, and at fifteen they take part. When we are with Kiwi friends and they are eating, they show respect for our ways.'

And with a wide spread of ages in the family, it has made sense to stick to the traditional Somali segregation during eating. At mealtimes, all the younger children sit together and eat first. Then the older children and the adults have their meal. When a male guest comes, he eats separately with the men, and the women eat later.

Marian would like to shop daily for fresh food, as she did in Somalia and in Kenya, where they spent some years as refugees, but says that's not the Kiwi way. 'When you go to the supermarket you buy food and it goes into the fridge for two or three days. Most shopping you do weekly, even though we are used to getting produce every day and it always being fresh.'

Marian is an accomplished cook and one of the family's favourites is her sweets. She'll sometimes spend a whole day making them. 'I can make many different sweets. I like things I can make with my hands. Mincemeat inside bread is a favourite. After Ramadan, you see different varieties of sweeties, all home-made.'

Marian's devotion to her family and preservation of Somalian cuisine takes up most of her day but she's not worried by it.

And at the end of the day, despite his refusal to take part in food preparation, Mohamed is happy to clean up. He smiles at his incredibly youthful wife and mother of nine and explains: 'The kitchen is for the beauty of the female.'

Nicky Owers

I think I'd always been a latent vegetarian

There's no hesitation when Nicky Owers is asked to nominate the most useful item in her kitchen. 'My husband,' she laughs. 'He gets home at six o'clock and asks me what he can do to help.'

Nicky, husband Deane Henderson, and 3-year-old son Blake are all vegans — they eat no animal products. Nicky turned vegetarian in her teens. 'I decided one day it was all too ghastly eating animals. I think I'd always been a latent vegetarian and if anyone in our family had been one and shown me that option, it might've dawned on me earlier.'

Having forsaken meat, Nicky and Deane opted for the vegan path while she was pregnant with Blake. 'We had friends who are vegans and we watched a video with them about dairy farm animals and it spelt out for us why we should be vegans. There is cruelty in the production of food. There is a detrimental effect on the environment in regard to run off, etc, and we just waste food anyway by cycling it through animals to us. All the herbicides and other -icides are another issue.'

As Nicky takes a freshly baked coconut loaf out of the oven, she explains there's not a lot of trouble associated with their choice of diet. 'Our local supermarket is very good. It stocks all the lentils and pulses we need. I buy our vegetables from Commonsense Organics. We also grow vegetables including silverbeet, carrots, lettuces, tomatoes, cape gooseberries and garlic.'

Nicky has some vegan cookbooks, but says substituting vegan ingredients for the eggs, butter, and other animal products found in many recipes isn't hard. The coconut loaf, for example, is just flour, raw sugar, coconut, vanilla essence and baking powder.

'You can buy a vegan cheese substitute, but my taste has changed now and I have lost the palate for that kind of food. Plus it's pretty expensive.'

Nicky spends a lot of time in the kitchen now she has Blake and another baby on the way. The kitchen refurbishment got underway when Blake was born and is not quite finished, but she loves the deep jade-green joinery and pale apricot walls.

'We don't eat out a lot, not because we're vegans, but because we have Blake and we are on one income now. When we are at home we are a hundred per cent committed to this vegan lifestyle, but we are flexible when we go out. We let our morals slide for an evening in restaurants and just eat vegetarian. When we go out to people's homes we don't make a fuss about food.'

Bernie Portenski

The fitter your body is, the less you crave rubbish and fatty foods

Slaving away over a hot stove just isn't Bernie Portenski's thing. But give her a hairdryer or a stationary bike and she's really cooking. The 50-year-old marathon champion and solo mother of 9-year-old Marie-Jo finds the kitchen a great place to combine her work as a hairdresser and her heavy training schedule. 'Most of the time I spend in the kitchen I have the television on and I am on my stationary bike, training. I do an hour at a time. I have been known to pedal away and stir a pot. At least I can keep an eye on things.'

Except when she's talking serious sports talk, most of Bernie's conversation is punctuated with husky peals of laughter. A former three-pack-a-day smoker, Bernie has transformed herself into an international marathon champion, culminating in winning the Masters section of the Boston Marathon. As the shampoo ad says, it didn't happen overnight, but it did happen. 'Being a hairdresser, I puffed, puffed, puffed all day when I didn't have scissors in my hands. And sometimes when I did!

'I was trying to lose weight at the same time as giving up smoking. Once I started putting on weight, I decided exercise was the key. But until I got competitive there wasn't a change of diet. Then I felt I should try everything to get a benefit.

'I have always been a good eater, and I normalised my eating habits. My biggest problem is keeping my intake down — I love food so much it can be a hard thing to do. But the fitter your body is the less you crave rubbish and fatty foods. Quite often we have fish, chicken and vegetables, and we put interesting salads together.

'Food is important if you are competing in any sport. Now you have marathon packs — food you eat in the middle of marathons. The relationship between food and performance is a science in itself.

'It's important that you cook well, like only just steaming foods so you don't lose vitamins and minerals. I eat a lot of fruit, and I like basic food, so I am not depriving myself of anything.'

The kitchen of Bernie's Waikanae home was renovated just before she bought the house three years ago. It's light and modern, and a cool avocado green.

The fridge and cupboard doors have pieces of paper tacked onto them. Bernie cracks up laughing again as she pulls a piece of paper off the wall. 'Sometimes my friends try to get me to cook. What's this one? "Don't Worry Christmas Cake." They really think I need help! My recipes are more likely to be splattered with tint than ingredients,' she adds, pointing to fading brown smears.

When Marie-Jo was little, the kitchen was her bathroom and Bernie relishes the memories of those baby days. 'Marie-Jo was bathed in the kitchen sink until she was about four. She loved the kitchen sink even when she couldn't fit in it anymore. I didn't have to bend down and there are lots of entertaining things for a child in the kitchen, like mugs and scrubbers. It's a great pacifier.'

Bernie makes no claims to being anything other than a basic cook, but her own recipe, Magic Running Muffins, has made it into a local celebrity cookbook. 'Most people think they are pretty bland. They have no butter or sugar, but they do have golden syrup, bananas, apricots, molasses, coconut, yoghurt, raisins and wholemeal flour. The secret is that you have to eat the whole tray, then go off and run a marathon!'

Anna Reed

I like a table full of people and food

Anna Reed's passions are her work and her home. Relaxing in her suburban Christchurch cottage, the 57-year-old mother of two, sex worker and sexual health educator says she's come a long way since her days as a 'trippy little hippie' on the Coromandel.

'I am extremely domesticated, possibly obsessively. I have places for things. I am envious of people who rearrange their houses. I like everything cleaned and cleared. I maintain if you have fresh flowers and clean floors you can get away with a lot!

'I like a table full of people and food. I love to make food for other people. What I cook depends on who is coming. I am into strong, succulent, saucy, savoury things!

'I like to sit around the table with friends and I like putting different types of people together — people who would not normally meet. I am having a prostitutes' collective Christmas party next week and we will have a huge range of people together, from MPs to sex workers — it's a great mix.'

Anna readily admits to delusions of grandeur on the home front. 'I have a gold cutlery set which looks beautiful with gold serving dishes and gold-rimmed glasses. My oak dining table can go from being a four-person to a seventeen-person size.' A twinkling chandelier caps the elegant dining area.

It's a far cry from Anna's hippie days. 'I cooked on an open fire for years. I didn't have cold water, even, for years; it had to come from streams and rivers. I got used to cooking for large numbers of people. As soon as you saw someone you'd gather up wood to get the fire going. I lived for a while at the Wilderland commune and I picked up a lot of ideas from other people there. I used to do ten-day fasts — I would drink only green tea, eat brown rice, and smoke cigarettes!' she laughs.

Anna has worked hard to preserve the cottage character of her house while making practical improvements. 'The kitchen was originally part of a lean-to. I've moved the kitchen more than once! It's staying put now because the electrician and plumber refuse to move it any more. Everything in it came from demolition yards, including the big picture window in the dining area. I like looking out into the garden. But I've discovered you should not put lead-light windows above the sink! There are seventy-eight separate little panes to clean.

'I have a very small surface to work on. I like to have big dinners so I have to be tidy. There is nowhere else to go with piles of plates and dishes, so I clean up as I go. I have never had a dishwasher or a microwave. I don't consider doing the dishes a chore and I don't trust the energy that drives a microwave.'

Anna's father has left a legacy of fond childhood memories of food and entertaining. 'My father was Polish, he did dinner parties of food no one else would eat, like baked hedgehogs. He made yogurt too, which was unheard of in those days. People were always nervous of what they were eating if they were invited home! My mother worked at Victoria University, and Dad used to encourage her to bring home specimens from the labs like huge squids so he could experiment and make something with them.'

Anna finds her work quite spiritual, something that is echoed in her views on food. 'I love sharing food. It's like sharing a celebration of your lives together and introducing something new you have found. It's nice to give someone their first taste of things.'

Evelyn Skinner

Wellness and digestion are tied to the selection of food

Despite a kitchen that 'drives me bananas', Evelyn Skinner is a committed cook, and has even turned out an award-winning dessert. It's nearly thirty years since Evelyn featured twice weekly on television's *Spot On* children's programme. Since then she's lived mostly in London, returning to New Zealand two years ago and moving into a tiny cliffside cottage at Eastbourne, with views across to the South Island. Now an osteopath, she's still full of the energy and enthusiasm that brimmed over on the small screen.

'I quite often cook for between ten and twenty people, and I have to get all the preparation done early because there is no bench space,' she sighs, surveying the small kitchen, which also doubles as her office. 'I have to do all the fiddly things the day before, such as the potatoes and the chopping, the topping and tailing.'

But Evelyn isn't interested in minimising the time she spends cooking. In fact, quite the opposite. 'A physiological event takes place in the body when you are preparing

food. Wellness and digestion are tied to the selection of food and the process of things like chopping. Certain enzymes are produced in the mouth, which enable you to digest the meal properly. One should think carefully about using convenience foods because of that. They just don't get the digestive system going.'

Convenience events too, such as pot-luck dinners, also get the thumbs down. 'I presume the principle is that this person who's invited you is so busy they can't manage the cooking. What they're really saying is they will provide you with a room but can't be bothered to cook for you. Something happens when you cook for people, and to give away that gift, that opportunity to give, through food, is very worrying to me.'

Evelyn says that despite her firm views on cooking, she's no puritan when it comes to time- and labour-saving devices. 'This is the first dishwasher I have had. It's wonderful, because I couldn't stack up dishes; there wasn't the room. And I adore things like this little portable blender. There is no merit spending time chopping something when you can whizz it in a few seconds. I don't have a sadomasochistic approach or a Protestant work ethic about that side of cooking!'

Though strongly committed to an organic GM-free diet, Evelyn is a pragmatist. 'I have a debate going on with myself about fat in food. The leaner we've got, the less flavour we have or the flavour has changed. But I hardly eat anything with fat anyway.'

Evelyn Skinner's passion for great-tasting food led her to enter, and win, a competition in 1999 to design a signature dessert for the new millennium. 'I think the thing that tickled me was the idea of something people might truly believe would take over from the pavlova. Intellectually, I thought, well, it's got to be everything the pavlova is not. So I decided it had to be organic because I see New Zealand in the second millennium being an organic paradise, not a pavlova paradise! I used ground macadamia nuts with eggs, and essentially it's a soufflé. And I used the gold kiwi fruit in a sauce with honey. It's gluten free, and sugar free, but I did bend when it came to a little bit of cream because it's just gorgeous. I love cream!'

Karen Soich

My love of preserving comes from my childhood

'**Most people have a one-dimensional** view of me. I am hugely domestic and always have been,' says Auckland lawyer Karen Soich. Karen's name has been linked with the rich, the famous, and the infamous, through both her personal and professional life. However, close friends and family have always known another side of Karen.

From the age of eleven, she started filling in journals with recipes and culinary secrets passed on by relatives and friends. She still adds to the third journal in the same neat handwriting.

Karen says that in her teens, instead of spending her money on the latest fashion trends, she would put French cookware on layby at Smith and Caughey's. 'It was my version of a glory box! As well as cooking, I'm also really keen on embroidery. I'm self-taught and half-way through quite a large tablecloth at present.' Karen produces her work in progress. Each stitch is perfect and it's hard to tell one side from the other.

The kitchen of her Grey Lynn home and office is a picture of absolute order; her collections of china, crystal and other kitchenware are displayed without a hint of clutter.

Without doubt, she says, the pantry is the delight of her life. 'It's full of things, but Neil [Roberts, her late former husband] always used to say there was nothing you could actually eat! But I could make any dish as I have everything here.'

Karen moved into the house four years ago and says the kitchen is pretty much as she found it. 'All I've had to do is fill the place up with things. The Italian dinner set was bought when I was with Neil. At the time the green and pink were quite different and I must be the only person who has decided on furnishing fabrics based on the colours of a dinner set!'

Karen is well known for her home-made preserves, especially her tamarillo chilli chutney. 'My love of preserving comes from my childhood. Although my grandmother died when I was only six, I vividly remember the smell of her preserves. She was a great person for having big afternoon teas, too. She died when I was little so I taught myself how to preserve.

'I have a friend who is also keen on chutneys, so one Christmas we decided we would make lovely baskets of our produce for everyone. So we cooked and preserved, bought baskets, straw, wrappings, ribbons and made a huge effort. But it cost such a lot we never did it again. But I do give away my preserves. I take a jar of chutney with me instead of wine when I go for dinner.

'I did learn some things about cooking from my mother. She is a clean, healthy cook. And I learned from another woman I met at university who was into the other side of cooking, like tongue in aspic and rich sauces. When I went flatting I did the sauce and casserole thing, like my mother's cooking, but now I prefer to marinade meats, with chilli and cayenne, of course. I'm a great believer in putting chilli into everything. It adds flavour where it's needed and covers up tastes you don't want to find.'

As well as her pure love of things domestic, Karen uses her culinary skills to oil the wheels within wheels of the entertainment industry. She often combines work with pleasure. 'I entertain a lot for both personal and political reasons. I invite people who might start a deal if put together in the right way. I give it a chance to work, but don't push it. I act for a lot of friends, you see, and people I socialise with tend to be people I am either working for or against, broadcasters, producers, that sort of person.

'I like to put people together. I make it clear it's an introduction, no more and no less. I have to keep things in boxes because I run the largest practice in pure entertainment law and everyone knows each other. I am very strict about how I schedule appointments; I make sure people don't dovetail where just knowing they were here would raise issues.

'I play mother. There is safety in sitting round a dining table; it's non-confrontational, a soft arena for discussion.'

Karen travels overseas frequently and says food is always a major purchase. 'I bring lots of food home when I travel overseas. You can buy most things here now, but before that I used to look like a refugee from Eastern Europe, I would have so many bits of food with me!'

All the work-cum-play means Karen takes good care of herself and occasionally has bio-cleansing spells. 'I'll go three days without wine, which means three days without socialising, really!'

As she looks around her sunny, calm domain, Karen concedes a small point of weakness on the home front. She can clean, and does, but says that when her cleaner has been 'the house really smiles!'

Pam
Spite

I had the cheek once to tell a lecturer how to cook rice!

Pam Spite has a simple philosophy on food and family. 'Everything that you feed well grows well, whether it's a vegetable or a child,' she asserts. A mother of two, qualified dietician, former restaurateur and now farmer's wife and homestay host, Pam's credentials are impeccable.

She and her husband, Wilson, live in an elegant imposing Oamaru-stone house, just outside Oamaru. Wilson came to the 300-acre farm with his parents in the 1940s and brought Pam, his much younger bride, to the farm fifteen years ago.

Pam quickly set about modernising the home, including the large farmhouse kitchen, with its 14-foot stud. 'I trained in Home Science at Otago University and did a kitchen design option with Tom Esplin. When I came here the kitchen did not work. One day we got up and took two tons of stone out of the wall in just one day. Wilson was on a scaffold and I was wheelbarrowing the stone to the steps and just tipping it out. We turned it into a galley kitchen by taking out a wall. The walls were

never plastered over, as this was a place for servants and it was considered adequate for them! When we had the place repainted, the painter said he'd plaster the wall but we said no, just paint over the stone.'

There are three ovens including a Rayburn, which heats the water and the house. 'If you live in a place like this the wood falls out of the trees, so why not have one?' Pam sensibly asserts.

Large meat dishes of different patterns line a high shelf and, apart from two large framed botanical prints, the walls are kept simple and bare. A large pulley, first used more than a century ago to help dry laundry, now displays a row of baskets and dried flowers.

Pam says the kitchen functions well while retaining its old charm and character. 'It works well. I always do my pastry on the marble, it's from an old wash stand, and in my next house I want another marble section for pastry. I have a large amount of bench space and plenty of storage. When you have farm workers you need somewhere where they can eat and you can work in the kitchen. I designed it so they could be at the table and get their dishes into the dishwasher without getting in my way.'

Pam was born in China to British parents and loves food of all kinds, including some from the place of her birth. 'A plain plate of rice with butter and salt and pepper, I think that's nice, good plain staple food. I had the cheek once to tell a lecturer how to cook rice! It didn't go down too well!' she chuckles as she sets about producing light fluffy omelettes for lunch.

'I love eating. I love all the different flavours. I was brought up on different foods, including Indian food. My mother could make the best curries I have ever had.

'I do a lot of stir-fries. I just love them. They are so quick. I always have oyster sauce on hand in the cupboard. I go to Christchurch to buy Chinese food and fresh noodles.'

Trips to Christchurch, Wellington and Auckland always include visits to cafés and restaurants as a break from cooking, but also to check on current trends. 'I like fine cooking, the way our best chefs are performing. They're using international influences and getting great results.

'I started out with French food and, while I still enjoy it, I don't do it as heavy these days. I use good old-fashioned things that work — in the pudding department, things like meringues. I make coffee walnut meringues, or something like a butterscotch pavlova. I never make anything plain, I always like to make it more interesting.'

For the last ten years, since reducing their holding in the farm to just 1.2 hectares, Pam and Wilson have been opening their house to paying guests; it's a chance for Pam to fire up the kitchen and really show off her culinary skills.

'I often do a starter of salad with salmon. We are near the Waitaki River and we have beautiful salmon. We have the most wonderful food in this country. I can also offer people whitebait or a mousse or something along those lines. We have soups in winter. I gather every field mushroom that grows!

'For a main course, I usually do beef, or something like lamb baked in the oven with paprika and spices.

'I always have home-bottled jars of raspberries or some other fruit and you can pulverise them with cream into something. I make my own chocolates, and keep them in the freezer. My walnut meringues are pretty popular too.

'I adore using figs. When our figs are green, I cut them in half, put sugar on them, grill them and put them on a fresh lamb chop. It's so simple, so stunning.

'I am inclined to put a pinch of sugar on things, it brings out the natural flavours and sweetness in tomatoes for example.

'I grow and use a lot of herbs, but it's not always the effect you want. I love doing oxtails and lamb shanks and I am fascinated by how popular they have become. It's a comfort thing. When you go away overseas, you always want things like a lamb chop and vegetables. We have embraced everything in this country; it's wonderful. But people always come back to things they know.'

As much as possible, Pam uses produce from her own garden. 'We have potatoes, broad beans, rhubarb, strawberries, barlotti beans. And twenty-five different types of lettuce. I sell them to different restaurants. We have a microclimate here that lets me grow them year round.

'We also have beautiful soil and it flavours our potatoes. The Jersey bennies are lovely. It's stunning to dig something out of the ground and put it into a pot and cook it. I love it.'

Pam's gone organic in the last few years. 'We don't use any sprays here. I realised that if I used spray I would break the natural food chain. The ladybirds, for example, don't get to eat the aphids so you don't get ladybirds anymore.'

Pam the foodie slips easily into Pam the dietician. 'I am worried about the takeaways and other rubbish people are eating. I think, gosh where are the greens? So many meals don't have them.'

Twenty years ago, Pam owned and ran a restaurant in Amberley called the Pepper Mill. A reminder of that previous life sits prominently on a sideboard in the kitchen. It's a collection of shiny, colourful pepper mills, mostly given by friends. 'I really enjoyed the restaurant, it was a great success. But I've also always been happy in my own kitchen. They're the heart of the home.'

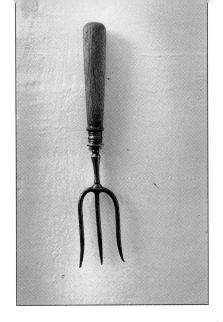

Cath Tizard
There is always a proper meal of meat or fish, and vegetables

Did New Zealand's first female Governor General, a highly practical woman, mother of five, with Scottish Presbyterian instincts, ever fend for herself during her five years at Government House? 'Get a grip! This is all I had to do,' she chuckles, snapping her fingers.

Dame Catherine Tizard admits to a substantial period of domestic readjustment when she left office and moved into her Herne Bay, Auckland apartment. 'It took me a while to get this kitchen into shape. I like things being tidy and orderly and strongly believe there is a place for everything. But I'd had stuff packed away for five years, I'd given a lot away and some had gone to the beach house. I had to start all over again, sorting things out. It was a bit like setting up a flat for the first time. All I had after Government House was a dining table, no chairs, a double bed and a chest of drawers.

'I hated this kitchen when I moved in. There is too much wasted space. But inertia has got in the way of changing it. I think about it all the time and will have it redone eventually. The sink, for example, is just wrong. It doesn't allow for a proper flow of dishes being stacked, washed, drained, and then put away.

Cath says the move to Government House was far less of an adjustment as she'd been in public life for years. However, she says the kitchen at Government House was very intimidating and she didn't go there often. 'The few times I did, I was very much the outsider and disrupted what was going on. The chefs and scullery maids would all come to attention, so it wasn't something I took to doing. My personal assistant handled all the liaison with kitchen staff in much the same way a wife would probably have done if I was a man.

'The hardest thing really was not to interfere. It was hard to make suggestions and say, "Look, let's do it differently." For example, during conversation with official visitors I always found it disruptive when the butler asked each of us individually whether we took milk and sugar in our tea and coffee. So I suggested we offer the milk and sugar and let them help themselves. But that is not the way it is done in those circles apparently, so the butler would not change his ways. In the end there was a compromise, but that involved someone else serving it my way, as he would not change for me.'

Cath is still very active in public life but likes to eat at home when she can. 'There is always a proper meal of meat or fish, and vegetables. It would be easier to make a piece of toast, but that's not for me. I was brought up on good nutrition.'

118

Jo Tyson

I keep my paint palette in the fridge

Nothing gives Jo Tyson more pleasure than the sight of a fresh fish sitting in her kitchen. Not that she plans to eat them, you understand. Her appreciation is that of an artist. A trained teacher and art scholar, Jo's kitchen doubles as her studio. As well as cooking for her husband and three children, Jo runs four adult and two children's art classes each week from home.

Dozens of students and possibly hundreds of fish, mainly trout, pass through her kitchen each year. 'I did the first fish as a gift for a friend in Wellington and it took off from there. I'm doing hundreds of fish now, mostly rainbow trout. People love the colour. But I prefer the brown trout myself; it's more subtle. Women buy them for their husbands. If they're not perfect, they don't go out because they're having a really critical eye go over them.'

Despite a sweeping view of Tasman Bay and Haulashore Island, Jo would love to move the art classes out of the kitchen. 'I dream of a studio, but we don't have the

money. It would mean I wouldn't have to clean up and clear everything away at the end of each class. That's why you can see piles of stuff all over the kitchen. I keep my paint palette in the fridge. It's quite clean, but people go to my fridge, and sometimes I can see them thinking "Oh, my God".'

As well as wanting the art out of the kitchen, Jo is also keen to cut back on the three meals a day routine. 'I used to love cooking but I am sick of it. It's three hundred and sixty-five dinners a year plus school lunches. I do so love food — I'd love not to be so sick of it,' she sighs.

'I have a repertoire, so we have Mexican tacos, pastas, enchiladas, and casseroles. I put a casserole on this morning during the art class. I think some of the women thought I'd got a beer out of the fridge because I was driven to it!'

A sketch by Jo of a proposed kitchen remake has pride of place on the fridge. As well as lobbying for a studio, she's trying to persuade husband Neil of the merits of her design. It would end the making-do she finds so frustrating.

'I want to be a real artist. I'm a bit like a production line with my fish! I think, however, that I am honing my painting skills while I'm doing this. And with a paintbrush in my hand, I'm singing! I have Kim Hill on or music going in the background and I'm happy.'

Roz Warner

I love the sunniness of the food — the lively vibrant flavours

On a sunny Marlborough day, sitting under the olive trees and sipping sangria, Roz Warner only has to close her eyes and she's back in her beloved Spain. After twenty years abroad, mostly in Spain, Roz has put down roots at Hawkesbury. Home is a tiny 150-year-old two-room cob cottage, her kitchen no bigger than a walk-in pantry.

Roz works happily in the limited space. 'You should only have to take one or two steps between the oven, the fridge and your bench. Obviously, I am a bit short of bench space, so when I am cooking for other people I just move a lot of things on the shelves into the shower box and use the shelves as benches. The mini-fridge came from a friend's caravan. I jokingly asked for it and they gave it to me. The desk it's under is a child's desk and that is my bench space. The bookshelf holds all my basic ingredients and the chest of drawers actually has mostly clothes in it! I take advantage of all the nooks and crannies to store jars and bottles.'

Roz is a professional cook, catering for local businesses on a private basis, and she's food consultant to a Marlborough winery. She learned how to cook from a friend who had restaurants in London and Seville; Mediterranean food is a clear favourite. 'I love the sunniness of the food — the lively vibrant flavours. Even if you are eating Mediterranean food on a dull day, it perks you up.'

Paella is her signature dish and she treasures a special paella pan, which can produce enough for twenty-five people. 'When I have people here we sit out the back under the trees and I make the paella over a real fire. But someone recently paid a thousand dollars for me to make them paella. I'd donated it as a prize for a winter wine charity auction. In Spain, it's often auctioned as a school fundraiser.'

She thinks the secret to good food is to keep it simple. 'You should use good ingredients and cook them simply. Dishes like spaghetti puttanesca are wonderful. But sometimes I spend an enormous amount of time on preparing food. Paella is a good example. You have to make the stock, shell the mussels, prepare the other ingredients. In Spain, you do it in a group among friends.'

Roz has been back in New Zealand for about five years now. She only came home for a break from London but decided to stay when she discovered that all her favourite ingredients, once considered exotic and therefore hard to get, were readily available here. 'When I left here in the 1960s you had to buy olive oil in the chemist shop! You can buy most things here now, or you can improvise. You can even buy big red novas, the chillis used in paella; the Kataia Fire people are drying them. It's amazing what you can find when you look around.'

Summer or winter, most weekends you'll find Roz entertaining friends at the back of the cottage. She says even the coldest days are bliss. 'A winter Sunday is beautiful and sunny here. We light a fire under the willows and it goes on until dark. If you're a bit chilly you just put another log on the fire.'

Francie *I have never made cheese on toast*
Shagin

Just two minutes' drive away from one of Marlborough's smallest kitchens, Roz's friend and part-time employer, Francie Shagin, happily admits her kitchen may seem 'over the top' but adds 'the best compliment I get is that people say it's homely.'

Francie and husband Terry moved to New Zealand in the early 1980s after living the fast life in Los Angeles, she as a retailer and he as a Hollywood lawyer. Diminutive Francie, four foot ten ('and a half, I'm hanging on to every half inch!'), somehow manages to fill her state-of-the-art 600-square metre kitchen by sheer force of personality and seemingly boundless energy.

The kitchen is an impressive blend of stainless steel and wood, dominated by an enormous granite island, shiny stainless steel rangehood, oversized wall clock, and a cavernous fireplace. One of Francie's favourite features is her 'comfort light' which subtly illuminates the pull-out pot shelves under the stove and throws a soft light across the floor. 'My mother always left a light on in the kitchen for us when we were kids in case we came down in the night.'

Francie's kitchen is a busy one. A self-taught cook, she now runs her business, an Epicurean Affair, from home, and holds classes there. For those sessions she has large mirrors hung over the benches so her students can easily see what she's doing. 'When people come, it's an entertainment really,' she says, pulling on white surgical gloves before demonstrating one of her tried-and-true simple recipes.

'There are two types of cooks. There are people who understand and can cater for large numbers, like forty. Roz is one of them. And there are people like me, for whom twelve is the maximum.

'I like to entertain impromptu, like throwing together risotto or pasta. I love Italian food and that's great because you can always have the staples in your pantry or fridge. We can have pasta or risotto five nights of the week. It's a one-pot meal, with salad and wine.

Francie is matter of fact about cooking. 'I do easy, I like easy! I really cook for Terry and me. I am a very lazy person really. I rely on Roz and Jeremy (another friend and accomplished chef) a lot, they're my kitchen fairies! But in thirty-one years of marriage, I have never made cheese on toast, for example, even if I haven't felt like cooking. On those days I will make a frittata, it's easy but lovely to eat.

'Terry is so cute. When I serve something up he always says, "Oh, I love this dish" even when he hasn't eaten it before.

'He's the clean-up man. I can't wake up to a dirty kitchen. When dinner's finished and there are lots of things to do, he just says, "Let's go to bed. I don't tell you how to cook, don't tell me how to clean." He gets up early, cleans up, and brings me a cup of tea and tomatoes on toast. It's such a New Zealand thing. None of my friends in America have their husbands bring them tea in bed.

'I love being here and I love the house. Terry goes away sometimes for a few nights, but I never feel like I am rattling around it. I feel this is our nest.'

Kerre
Woodham
I cook every day, often four meals

One of New Zealand's great party girls has finally been tamed. For the first time, Kerre Woodham is uttering the previously unthinkable L-word — love. And she's settling in to a life of domestic bliss. Sitting in the sunny Auckland kitchen in the home she shares with daughter Kate and partner Tom, she glows with pride about her new life and loves. Her smile competes with that of a beaming fat Buddha, bought on a trip to Hong Kong and now a good luck charm for her and Tom.

The piss-fairy, so often referred to in her witty *Metro* columns, has stopped waving her wand and ginger beer is now the drug of choice. 'I've had years of partying and playing up. But there are only so many parties you can go to and now I love being home. Life has always just happened to me and I've taken part enthusiastically. I'm currently working all the hours God sends, which I cannot believe, and all I yearn to do at night is sit at home with the family.

'I feel very womanly cooking for Tom. He really loves and appreciates everything

I cook, so it's a real pleasure. It's funny that I've only recently learned to cook, as most people associate me with food and cooking from my time waitressing and on the cooking programme. I think maybe they think of me and food because I'm round! I love that, and all those round words like "fecund" — it's a giving sort of thing.

'I cook every day, often four meals. I have to have something to take in to work [night-time talkback], I cook for Tom, Kate needs something different as she's vegetarian on and off, and then there are the cats. They're really picky eaters, especially Geri [named by Kate for Geri Halliwell of Spice Girls fame].

'Being a late convert to domestic life is great. I've gone from being the most useless creature in the kitchen to knowing a few reliable things off by heart and enjoying experimenting. Soup is my favourite. I recently splashed out on a very big expensive Le Crueset pot for my soups and even Tom agrees anything that comes out of that pot is delicious. I've also learned how to cook a real risotto.

'I don't mind really that it's so time consuming. I think that's a woman thing. Women have to have lots of things on the go at the one time. So when I am here cooking, I have the radio on and I'm listening for issues for the talkback, I'm talking to Tom about his day, helping with Kate's homework and fielding phone calls too.

'But the best part of the night is when work is over and I drive home. The family are tucked up in bed, Tom's left the light on and the garage door is open. What more could I ask for?'

Jane Young

Everyone congregates in here around the table, despite all the clutter

'**Basically my life revolves** around dressing up, and eating and drinking!' laughs television reporter Jane Young. The kitchen of her Wellington villa is, in more ways than one, the engine room of a frenetic social and family life. Jane's fridge magnet sums up the woman: 'Dull Women Have Immaculate Kitchens.' Jane has been called many things, but never dull, and her Wellington kitchen is, well, not exactly immaculate.

When she's not crossing live from Parliament during peak time television news bulletins, or on the road covering election campaigns, Jane can be found, more often than not, in the kitchen, churning out both *haute cuisine* and *haute couture*.

'Everything happens in here,' she says, surveying the apple-green walls decorated with large framed paintings by 7-year-old daughter Lucy. It's not the kitchen itself that is noteworthy but rather the storm of activity within. 'I cook here, I sew here, I always have the cell phone on for calls from work, Lucy plays with her Barbies, friends eat and drink. Sometimes it's all go all at the same time.'

The dining table is testimony to this domestic hyperactivity. It is permanent home to a state-of-the-art sewing machine and overlocker, piles of exquisite fabrics, *Cuisine* magazines, *Vogue* patterns, Lucy's schoolwork, and press releases spilling out of a stylish briefcase. Behind the overloaded table is a large stand-alone pantry, piled precariously with dozens of huge ceramic platters and bowls. It soon becomes clear they're not just there for effect. 'I really like throwing impromptu dinners or really large dinner parties. That's why the pantry is always groaning with stuff.'

She caters single-handedly for parties of up to seventy but wouldn't dream of resorting to sausage rolls, or buying in food. 'Everyone congregates in here around the table, despite all the clutter. We even eat around the sewing machines, as there's always something on the production line.' She points to a tailor's dummy sporting a sequinned ball dress, and to a coat and a suit, hanging by the door, both nearly finished.

'I like people being in the kitchen with me, but I'd rather they sat with a drink and talked to me, whatever I'm doing. Clearly they can't help out with the sewing, and it's pretty much the same when I'm cooking because it's all in my head.'

Mostly, Jane says, she just makes up dishes depending on what's seasonal and what's in the cupboards. She claims never to have had a flop, but admits to occasional improvisation when something has not quite worked out.

The single mother of two (her son Aaron is 18) says life has always been busy but she's been blessed with children who just fit in with her hectic lifestyle. In fact, Lucy has turned her mother's obsession with fine clothes to her own advantage. 'When I make something to wear, Barbie gets a miniature copy of it. And whether I've just made myself and Barbie new ball gowns, Lucy just calls them Barbie's T-shirts!'

While she resists the Superwoman tag, she gets by on little sleep and her Southland-bred metabolism is immune to hangovers. And tucked away in a corner of the kitchen is a motorised treadmill, on which she also works out for an hour a day. 'If people ask me how I can be bothered doing all this, I don't even get the question. I love being busy, whether it's exercise, sewing, cooking, or putting in a hard day at work.'

Sylvia Zonoobi
Sometimes we cook food without a name!

When Sylvia Zonoobi's marriage to her Iraqi husband ended, she was left with three wonderful assets. Two of them are daughters Jasyl and Hasyl, and the third is a mastery of exotic Persian cuisine.

A Filipino, Sylvia has lived in New Zealand for ten years. She became stranded here during the Gulf War while on a holiday. Her visa had expired, and no airline wanted to know about her, so she applied for asylum. After a separation of three and a half years, Jasyl and Hasyl were reunited with their mother, and the three of them live in her small Wellington council flat with her new partner, Machu, also an Iraqi.

Sylvia has a bubbly personality and life revolves around family, food, the church and hospitality. 'This home loves food. We don't smoke, we don't drink, and so food is the most important thing to us.

'Most of the time we cook Persian food which I learned to cook while in Iraq,' she says, reaching for some small round containers of saffron. 'Machu's parents sent it because it's too expensive to buy here.' Sylvia says that according to legend, saffron must be used with care. 'You mustn't use too much because it makes you laugh,' she giggles. You get the sense that Sylvia uses a lot of saffron.

As well as Persian cuisine, there are other family favourites. 'We love fish in this house. It's very expensive though; I wonder how come, because New Zealand has so much water all around. In the Philippines if you eat fish, it means you are from a poor place, but not here. Sometimes we eat crab; it's my favourite, but my family aren't so keen.

'We have rice for breakfast with fried egg or leftovers. We eat a lot of vegetables and not so much meat. Occasionally we have roasts. And sometimes we cook food without a name! We don't use a recipe, and it usually works out. We have a good appetite!'

On Sundays after Mass, Sylvia and other Filipinos are able to buy traditional breads and savouries. Two churches take turns supplying the food. 'Our bread is a little sweeter and has a more cake-like texture than Kiwi bread. It's also flavoured with things like cheese, or mango and yam powder.'

Sylvia loves her modest kitchen because it is bright, with no curtains to block the light or to clean. 'And another thing I like about my kitchen is that I can see out of my window onto the street. People tell me they go past, and look in, and can see me, sometimes eating or working.'

Sylvia loves to know exactly what's going on around her whether on the street or in her own home. 'I keep a mirror by the kitchen window because I don't like having my back to everyone in the house or not seeing who is coming through the door. While you're doing the washing up you can have a good look!' she says, grinning broadly.

Clare
de Lore

Born in Christchurch, the second of Moya and Jim de Lore's four children, Clare de Lore set her sights on a career in journalism from an early age. Completing a diploma in journalism in 1977, she worked for both private and public radio for fifteen years. For seven years she was a political reporter for Radio New Zealand News in the parliamentary press gallery, and chairperson of the press gallery for two of those years. Clare was communications adviser to the State Services Commissioner and ran a public relations consultancy for two years before leaving the full-time workforce in 1996. She was relieving producer on the Kim Hill programme in 1996 and 1997. On a voluntary basis she has been involved with Amnesty International.

Since marrying Don McKinnon in 1995, she has split her time between Wellington and Auckland, and frequent overseas travel. Her son James was born in 1998 and the family moved to London in March 2000 when Don took up the position of Commonwealth Secretary General.

Until researching and writing this book, Clare says she regarded herself as a reasonably good cook. Having interviewed some extraordinarily good cooks in the course of writing this book, she's not so sure. She consoles herself with the hope of fame and fortune as someone who writes about women, their cooking, their families, their lives and their dreams. Clare plans to enrol in some cooking classes as well as continuing her writing career in London.

Julia
Brooke-White

By her own definition, 1999 was a watershed year in photographer Julia Brooke-White's domestic life. Her 1870 Wellington house received its first kitchen makeover, leaping more than a century in design and function.

However, Julia's refusing to be enticed into spending more time slaving over a hot stove. She's embarked on a new eating regime, simplifying her diet, eliminating meal time decision-making and shopping, which she hates. In the twenty-first century, Julia's breakfast will always be either homemade muesli or porridge; lunch, Vogel's toast, with either avocado, pesto or cottage cheese; and dinner will be on the hoof, as she grazes around her bountiful garden. If pushed she might steam some vegetables.

The mother of two adult daughters, Echo and Marigold, Julia's previous careers have been as a bacteriologist, weaver, wool classer, and sailor. A professional photographer for ten years, she has worked on two other books, *Hokitika Handmade* and *Yalo I Viti*. Having specialised in art and craft photography, Julia immensely enjoyed the human contact involved in recording the images in this book.